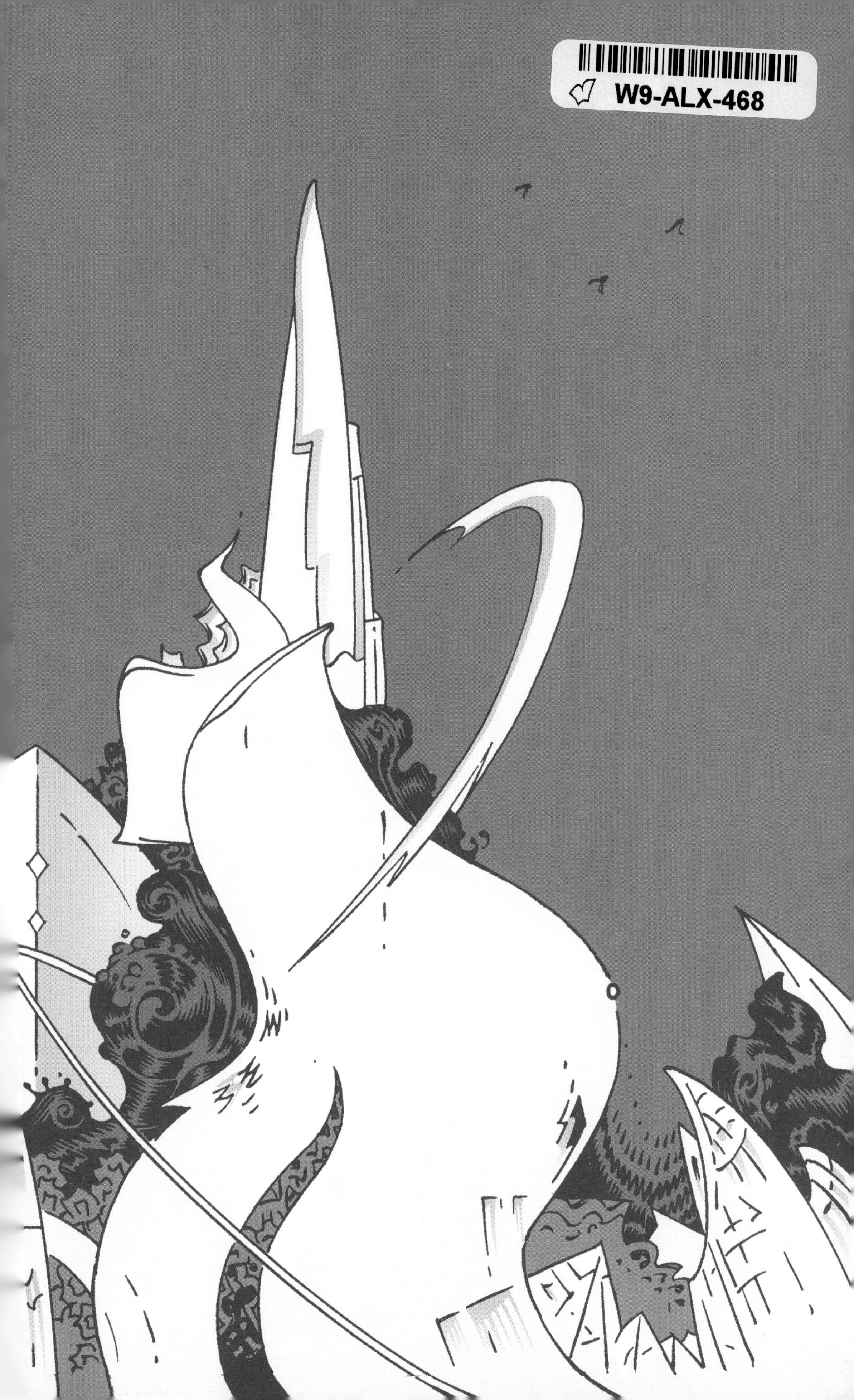

NEIL GAIMAN'S
Murder Mysteries™

ADAPTED FOR COMICS
by
P. CRAIG RUSSELL

OP. 51

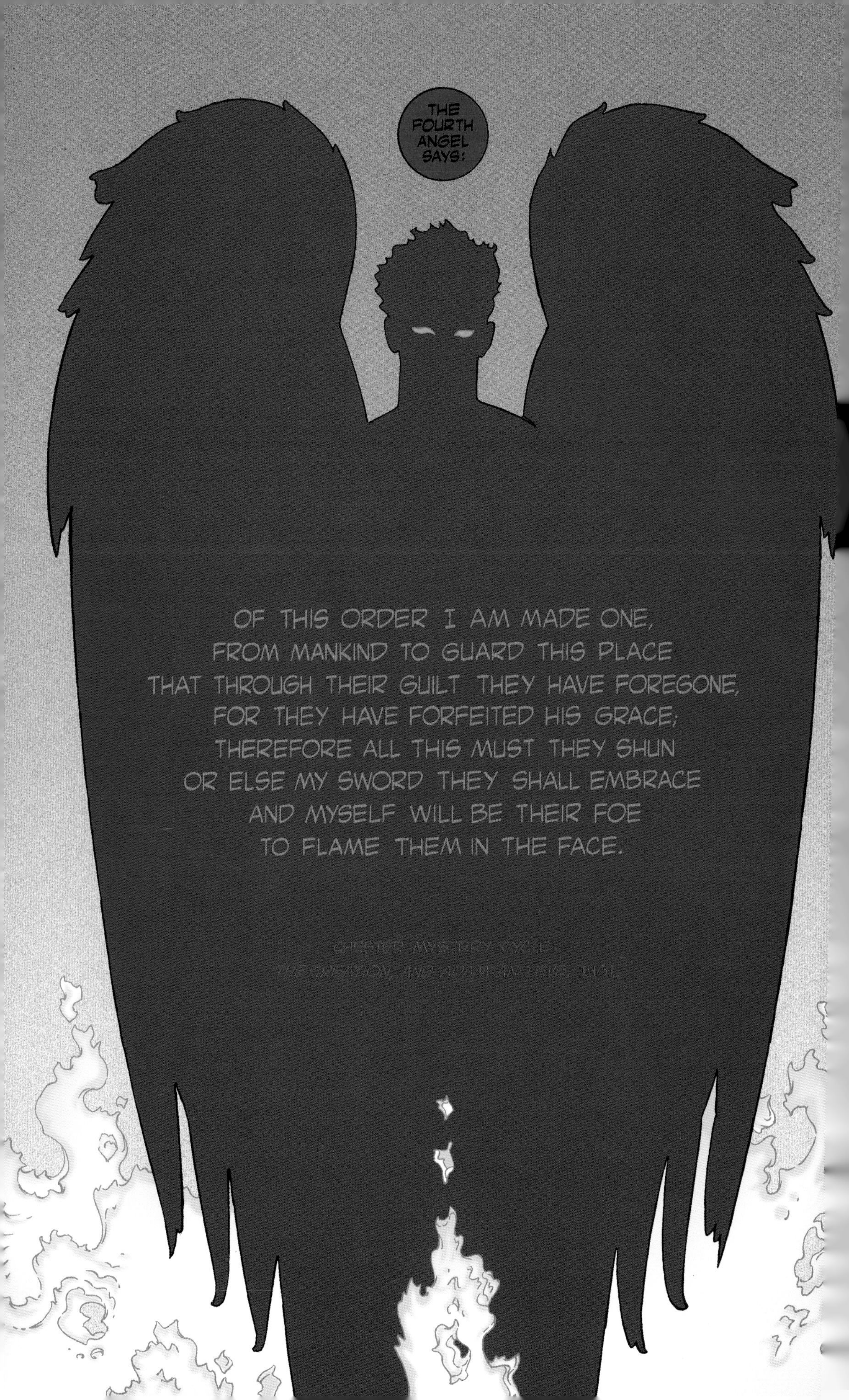
THE FOURTH ANGEL SAYS:
OF THIS ORDER I AM MADE ONE,
FROM MANKIND TO GUARD THIS PLACE
THAT THROUGH THEIR GUILT THEY HAVE FOREGONE,
FOR THEY HAVE FORFEITED HIS GRACE;
THEREFORE ALL THIS MUST THEY SHUN
OR ELSE MY SWORD THEY SHALL EMBRACE
AND MYSELF WILL BE THEIR FOE
TO FLAME THEM IN THE FACE.
CHESTER MYSTERY CYCLE:
THE CREATION, AND ADAM AND EVE, 1461.

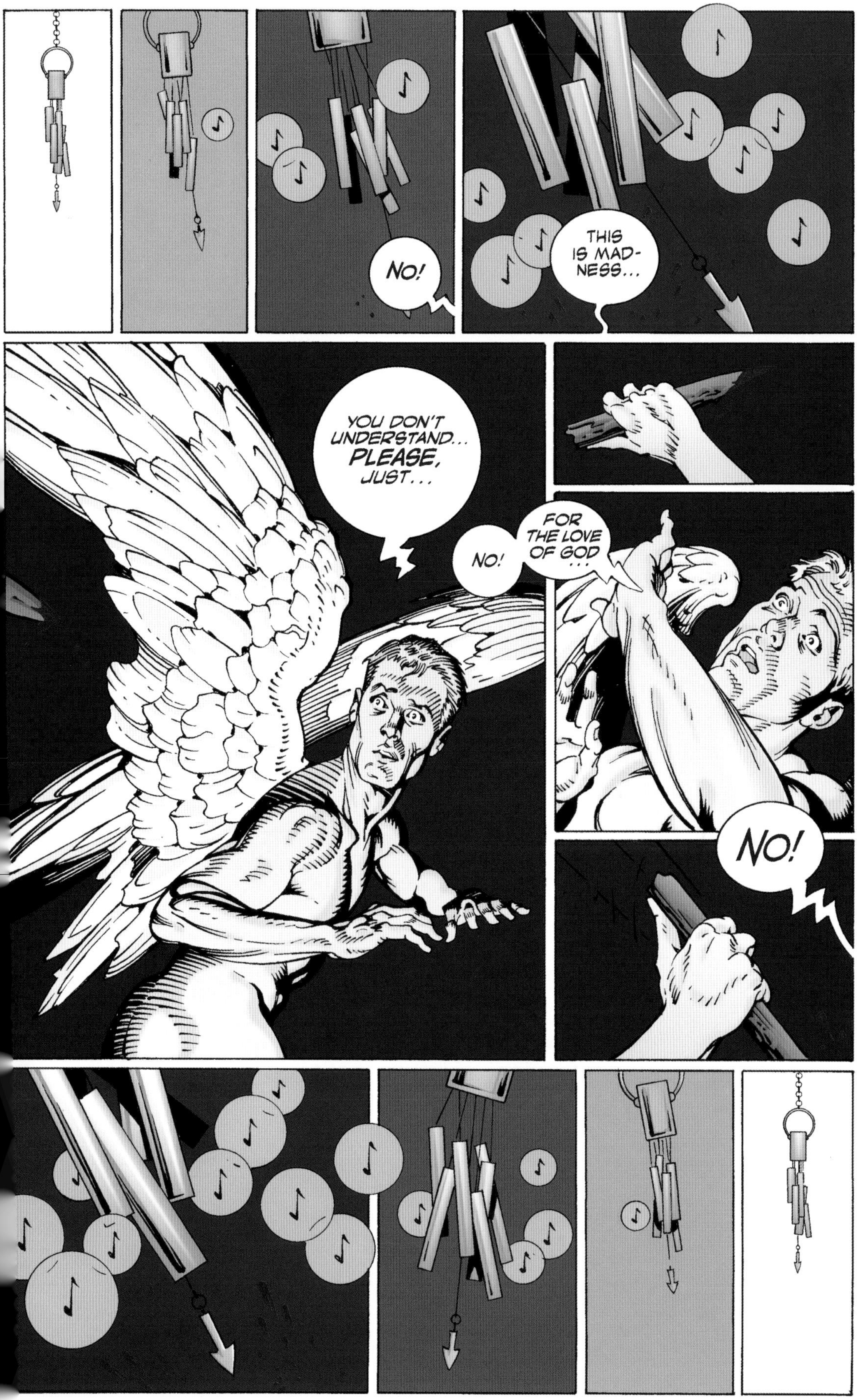
NO!
THIS IS MAD-NESS...
YOU DON'T UNDERSTAND... PLEASE, JUST...
NO!
FOR THE LOVE OF GOD...
NO!

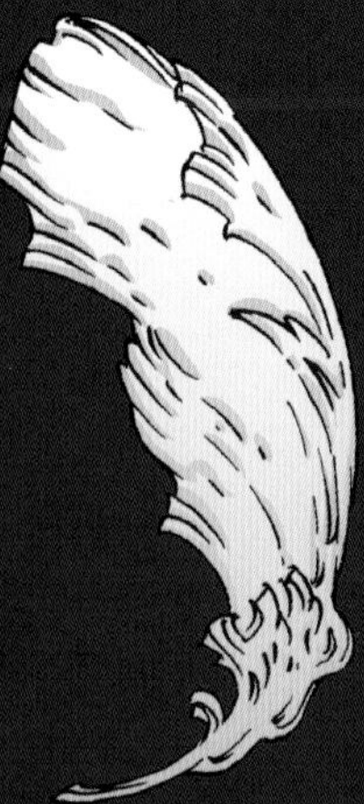

ORIGINAL SHORT STORY AND RADIO PLAY
NEIL GAIMAN
○
GRAPHIC STORY SCRIPT AND ART
P. CRAIG RUSSELL
○
COLORING
LOVERN KINDZIERSKI
○
LETTERING
GALEN SHOWMAN
○
EDITOR
SCOTT ALLIE
○
PUBLISHER
MIKE RICHARDSON

Neil Gaiman's Murder Mysteries™, June 2002. Published by Dark Horse Comics, Inc., 10956 SE Main Street, Milwaukie, Oregon 97222. Text © 2002 Neil Gaiman. Adaptation and illustrations © 2002 P. Craig Russell. Dark Horse Maverick™ is a trademark of Dark Horse Comics, Inc. Dark Horse Comics® and the Dark Horse logo are trademarks of Dark Horse Comics, Inc., registered in various categories and countries. All right reserved. No portion of this publication may be reproduced or transmitted, in any form or by any means, without the express written permissio of Dark Horse Comics, Inc. Names, characters, places, and incidents featured in this publication either are the product of the author's imagination or are used fictitiously. Any resemblance to actual persons (living or dead), events, institutions, or locales, without satiric intent, is coincidenta

FIRST PRINTING   ISBN: 1-56971-634-X   PRINTED IN CHINA   VISIT P. CRAIG RUSSELL AT WWW.LURID.COM

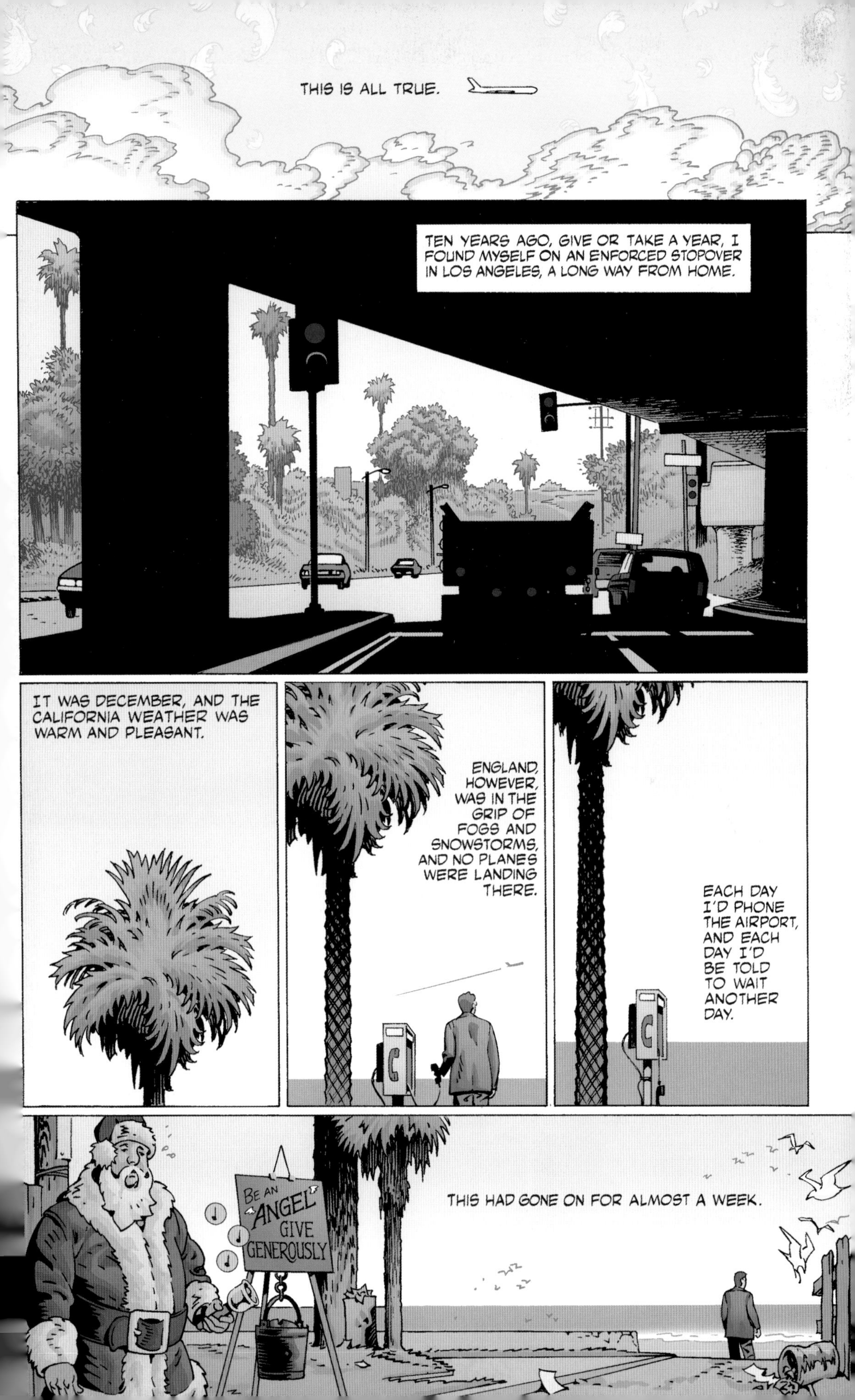
THIS IS ALL TRUE.
TEN YEARS AGO, GIVE OR TAKE A YEAR, I FOUND MYSELF ON AN ENFORCED STOPOVER IN LOS ANGELES, A LONG WAY FROM HOME.
IT WAS DECEMBER, AND THE CALIFORNIA WEATHER WAS WARM AND PLEASANT.
ENGLAND, HOWEVER, WAS IN THE GRIP OF FOGS AND SNOWSTORMS, AND NO PLANES WERE LANDING THERE.
EACH DAY I'D PHONE THE AIRPORT, AND EACH DAY I'D BE TOLD TO WAIT ANOTHER DAY.
BE AN ANGEL GIVE GENEROUSLY
THIS HAD GONE ON FOR ALMOST A WEEK.

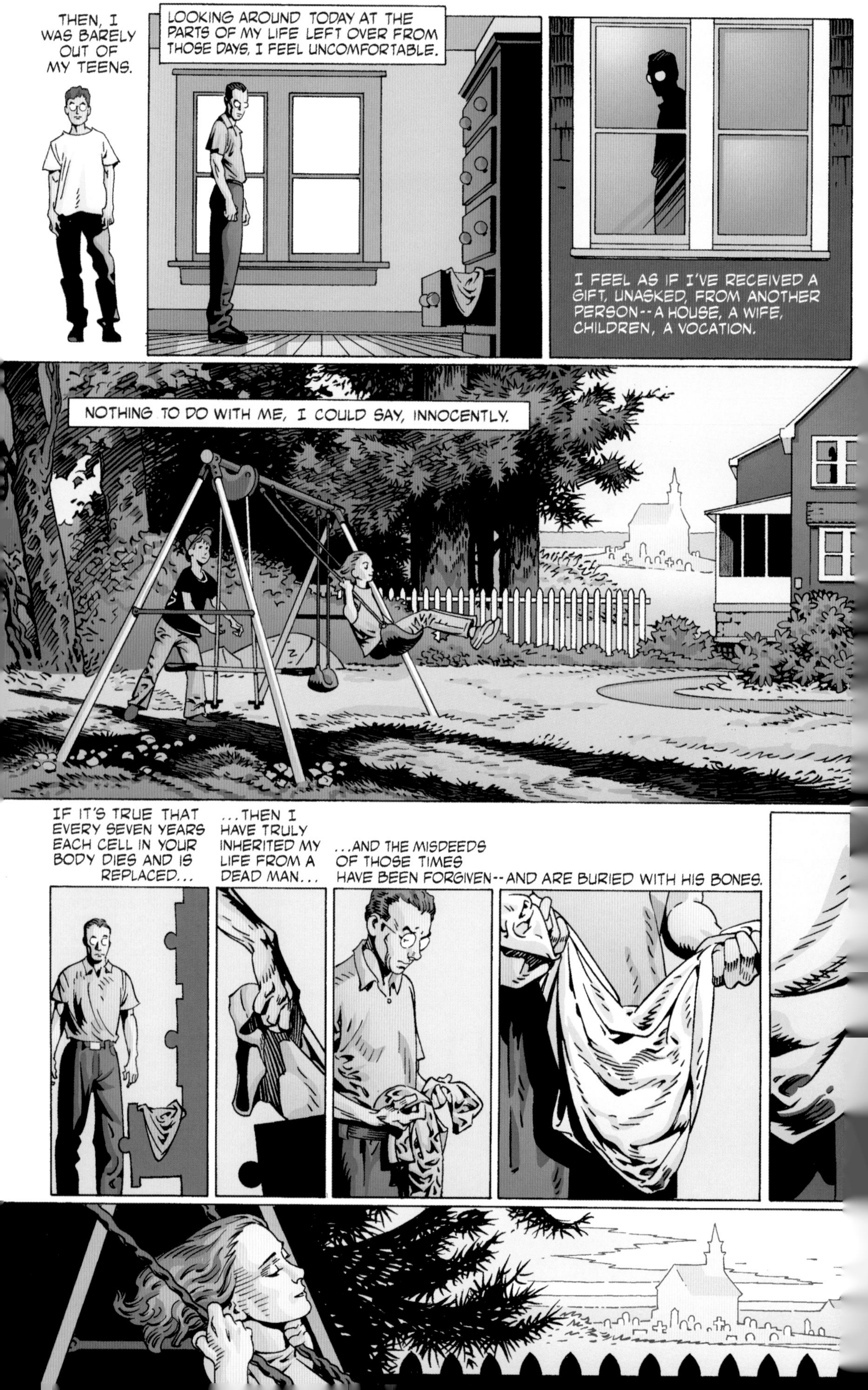
THEN, I WAS BARELY OUT OF MY TEENS.
LOOKING AROUND TODAY AT THE PARTS OF MY LIFE LEFT OVER FROM THOSE DAYS, I FEEL UNCOMFORTABLE.
I FEEL AS IF I'VE RECEIVED A GIFT, UNASKED, FROM ANOTHER PERSON--A HOUSE, A WIFE, CHILDREN, A VOCATION.
NOTHING TO DO WITH ME, I COULD SAY, INNOCENTLY.
IF IT'S TRUE THAT EVERY SEVEN YEARS EACH CELL IN YOUR BODY DIES AND IS REPLACED...
...THEN I HAVE TRULY INHERITED MY LIFE FROM A DEAD MAN...
...AND THE MISDEEDS OF THOSE TIMES HAVE BEEN FORGIVEN--AND ARE BURIED WITH HIS BONES.

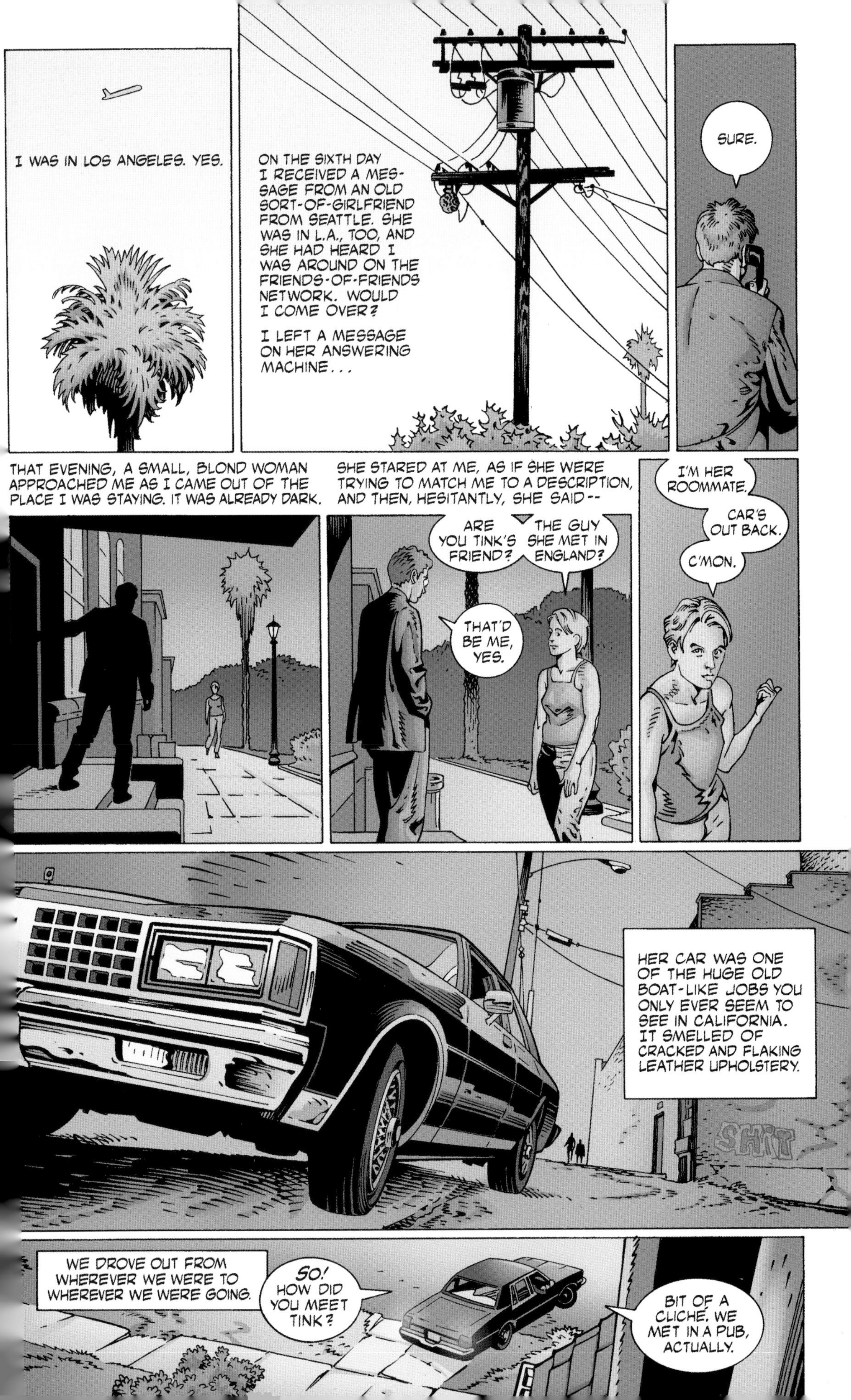
I WAS IN LOS ANGELES. YES.
ON THE SIXTH DAY I RECEIVED A MESSAGE FROM AN OLD SORT-OF-GIRLFRIEND FROM SEATTLE. SHE WAS IN L.A., TOO, AND SHE HAD HEARD I WAS AROUND ON THE FRIENDS-OF-FRIENDS NETWORK. WOULD I COME OVER?
I LEFT A MESSAGE ON HER ANSWERING MACHINE . . .
SURE.
THAT EVENING, A SMALL, BLOND WOMAN APPROACHED ME AS I CAME OUT OF THE PLACE I WAS STAYING. IT WAS ALREADY DARK.
SHE STARED AT ME, AS IF SHE WERE TRYING TO MATCH ME TO A DESCRIPTION, AND THEN, HESITANTLY, SHE SAID--
ARE YOU TINK'S FRIEND?
THE GUY SHE MET IN ENGLAND?
THAT'D BE ME, YES.
I'M HER ROOMMATE.
CAR'S OUT BACK.
C'MON.
HER CAR WAS ONE OF THE HUGE OLD BOAT-LIKE JOBS YOU ONLY EVER SEEM TO SEE IN CALIFORNIA. IT SMELLED OF CRACKED AND FLAKING LEATHER UPHOLSTERY.
SHIT
WE DROVE OUT FROM WHEREVER WE WERE TO WHEREVER WE WERE GOING.
SO! HOW DID YOU MEET TINK?
BIT OF A CLICHÉ. WE MET IN A PUB, ACTUALLY.

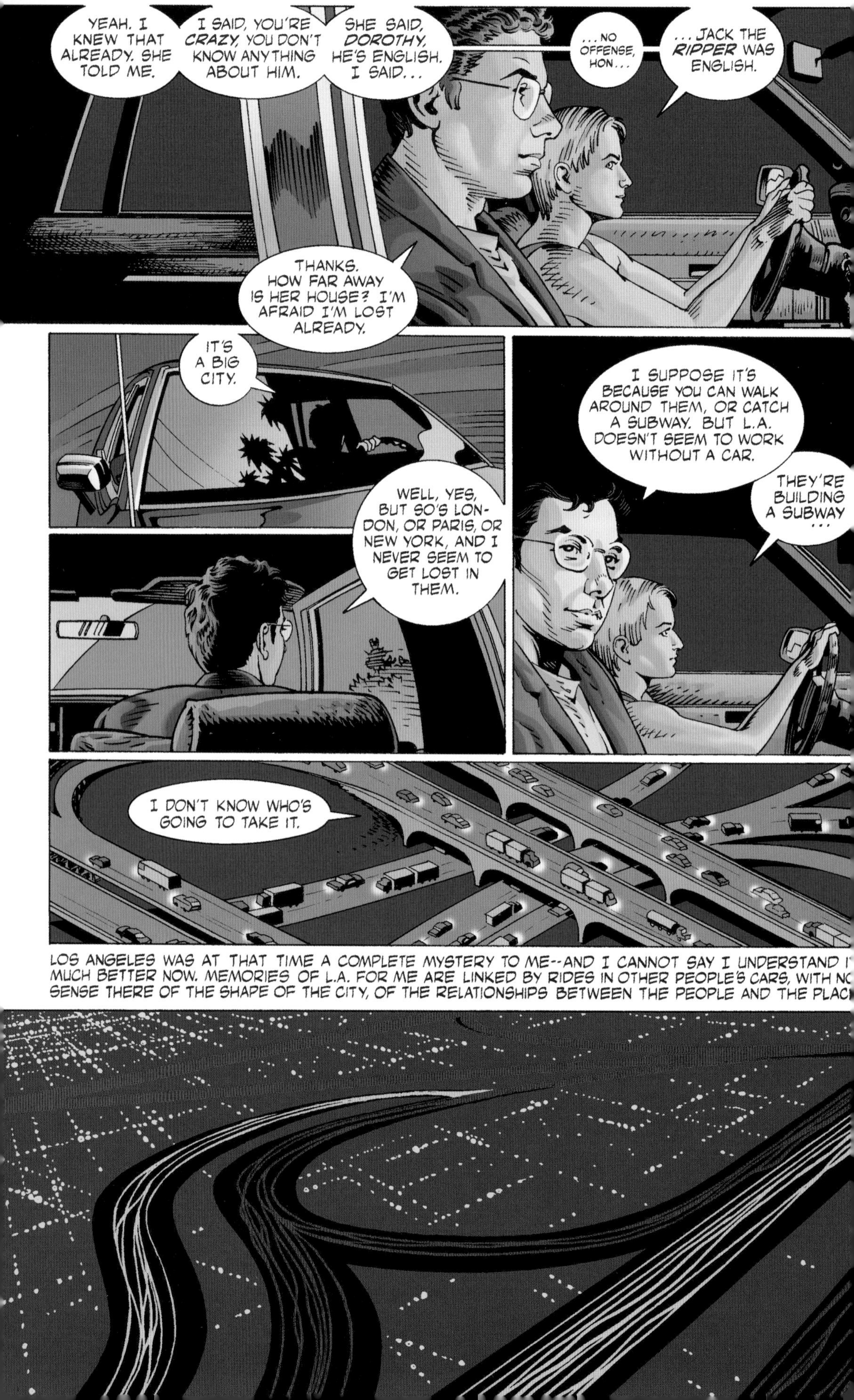
YEAH. I KNEW THAT ALREADY. SHE TOLD ME.
I SAID, YOU'RE *CRAZY,* YOU DON'T KNOW ANYTHING ABOUT HIM.
SHE SAID, *DOROTHY,* HE'S ENGLISH. I SAID...
...NO OFFENSE, HON...
...JACK THE *RIPPER* WAS ENGLISH.
THANKS. HOW FAR AWAY IS HER HOUSE? I'M AFRAID I'M LOST ALREADY.
IT'S A BIG CITY.
WELL, YES, BUT SO'S LON-DON, OR PARIS, OR NEW YORK, AND I NEVER SEEM TO GET LOST IN THEM.
I SUPPOSE IT'S BECAUSE YOU CAN WALK AROUND THEM, OR CATCH A SUBWAY. BUT L.A. DOESN'T SEEM TO WORK WITHOUT A CAR.
THEY'RE BUILDING A SUBWAY...
I DON'T KNOW WHO'S GOING TO TAKE IT.
LOS ANGELES WAS AT THAT TIME A COMPLETE MYSTERY TO ME--AND I CANNOT SAY I UNDERSTAND I
MUCH BETTER NOW. MEMORIES OF L.A. FOR ME ARE LINKED BY RIDES IN OTHER PEOPLE'S CARS, WITH N
SENSE THERE OF THE SHAPE OF THE CITY, OF THE RELATIONSHIPS BETWEEN THE PEOPLE AND THE PLAC

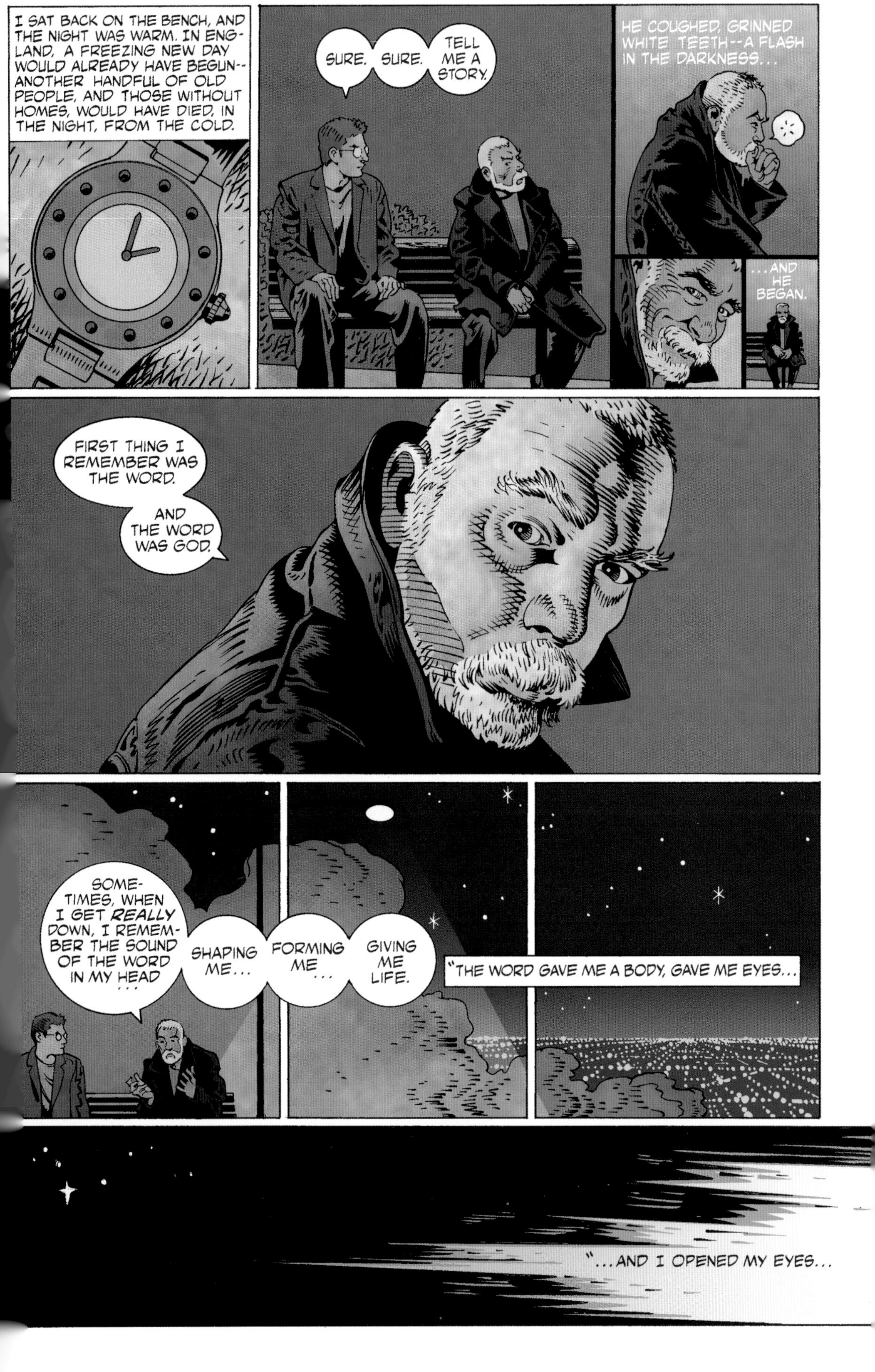
I SAT BACK ON THE BENCH, AND THE NIGHT WAS WARM. IN ENGLAND, A FREEZING NEW DAY WOULD ALREADY HAVE BEGUN--ANOTHER HANDFUL OF OLD PEOPLE, AND THOSE WITHOUT HOMES, WOULD HAVE DIED, IN THE NIGHT, FROM THE COLD.
SURE.
SURE.
TELL ME A STORY.
HE COUGHED, GRINNED WHITE TEETH--A FLASH IN THE DARKNESS...
...AND HE BEGAN.
FIRST THING I REMEMBER WAS THE WORD.
AND THE WORD WAS GOD.
SOMETIMES, WHEN I GET *REALLY* DOWN, I REMEMBER THE SOUND OF THE WORD IN MY HEAD...
SHAPING ME...
FORMING ME...
GIVING ME LIFE.
"THE WORD GAVE ME A BODY, GAVE ME EYES...
"...AND I OPENED MY EYES...

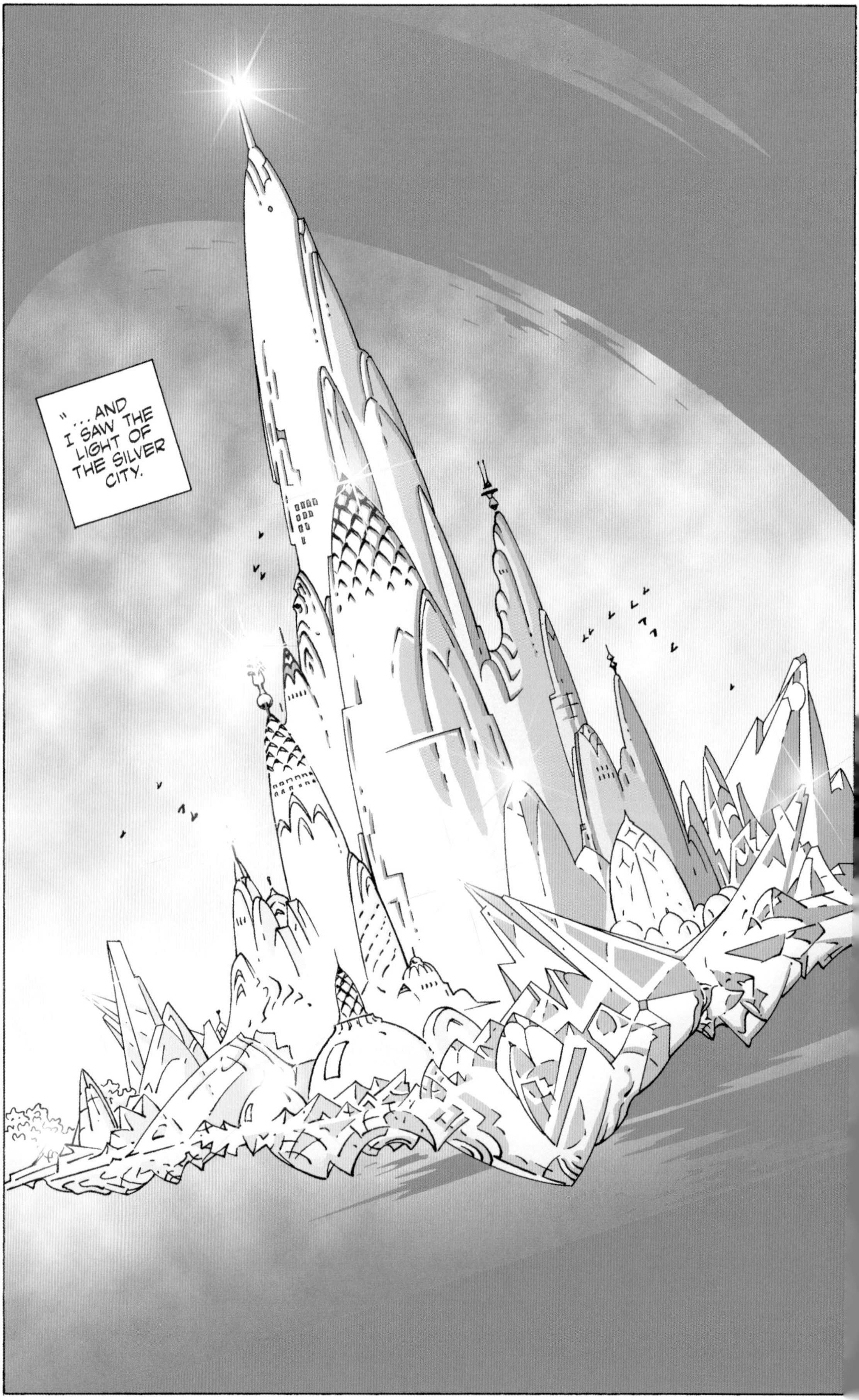
"...AND I SAW THE LIGHT OF THE SILVER CITY.

"I WAS IN A ROOM--A SILVER ROOM-- AND THERE WASN'T ANYTHING IN IT, EXCEPT ME.

"IN FRONT OF ME WAS A WINDOW, THAT WENT FROM FLOOR TO CEILING, OPEN TO THE SKY...

"... AND THROUGH THE WINDOW I COULD SEE THE SPIRES OF THE CITY...

"... AND AT THE EDGE OF THE CITY, THE DARK.

"I DON'T KNOW HOW LONG I WAITED THERE. I WASN'T IMPATIENT OR ANY- THING, THOUGH. I REMEMBER THAT.

"IT WAS LIKE I WAS WAITING UNTIL I WAS CALLED, AND I KNEW THAT SOMETIME I WOULD BE CALLED. AND IF I HAD TO WAIT UNTIL THE END OF EVERYTHING, AND NEVER BE CALLED, WHY, THAT WAS FINE TOO. BUT I'D BE CALLED, I WAS CERTAIN OF THAT. AND THEN I'D KNOW MY NAME, AND MY FUNCTION."

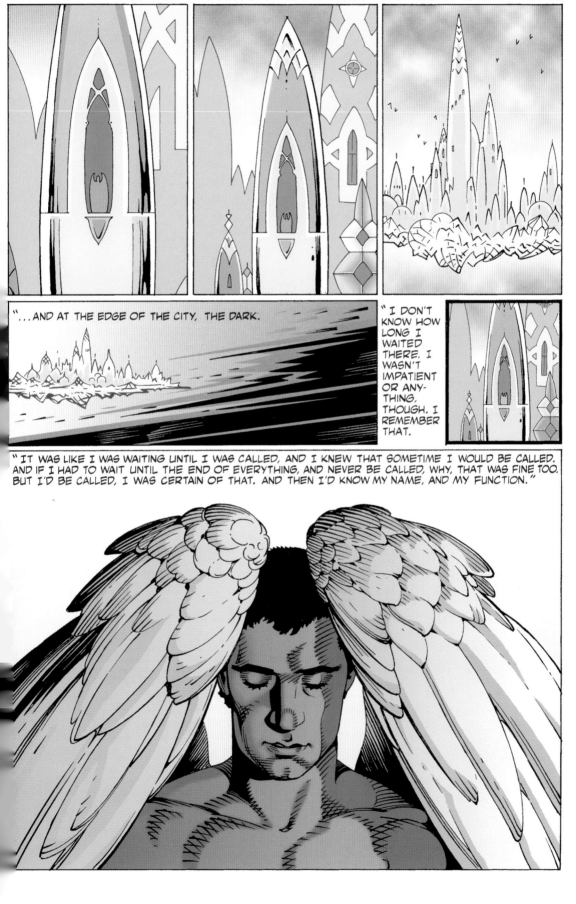

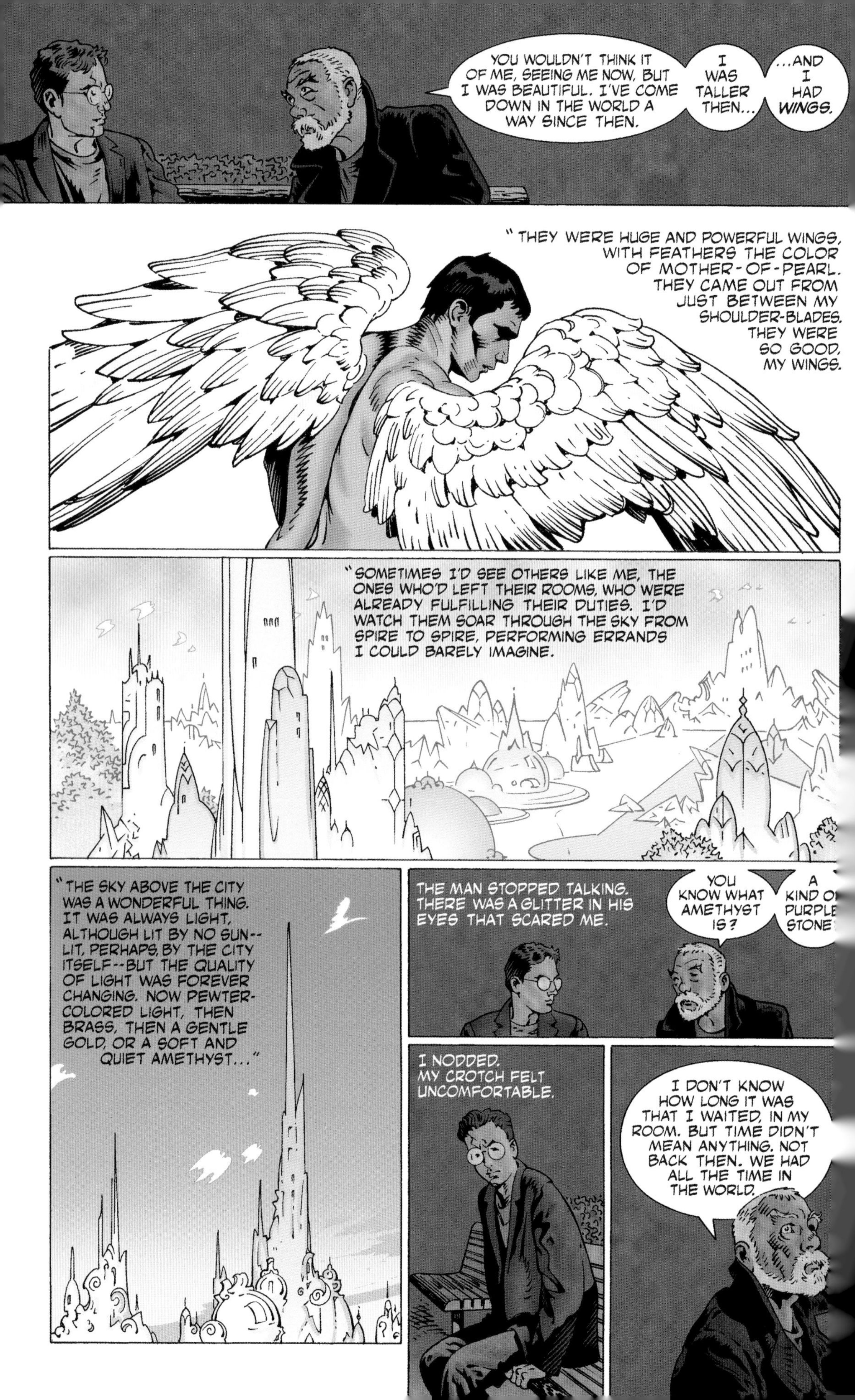
YOU WOULDN'T THINK IT OF ME, SEEING ME NOW, BUT I WAS BEAUTIFUL. I'VE COME DOWN IN THE WORLD A WAY SINCE THEN.
I WAS TALLER THEN...
...AND I HAD WINGS.
"THEY WERE HUGE AND POWERFUL WINGS, WITH FEATHERS THE COLOR OF MOTHER-OF-PEARL. THEY CAME OUT FROM JUST BETWEEN MY SHOULDER-BLADES. THEY WERE SO GOOD, MY WINGS.
"SOMETIMES I'D SEE OTHERS LIKE ME, THE ONES WHO'D LEFT THEIR ROOMS, WHO WERE ALREADY FULFILLING THEIR DUTIES. I'D WATCH THEM SOAR THROUGH THE SKY FROM SPIRE TO SPIRE, PERFORMING ERRANDS I COULD BARELY IMAGINE.
"THE SKY ABOVE THE CITY WAS A WONDERFUL THING. IT WAS ALWAYS LIGHT, ALTHOUGH LIT BY NO SUN--LIT, PERHAPS, BY THE CITY ITSELF--BUT THE QUALITY OF LIGHT WAS FOREVER CHANGING. NOW PEWTER-COLORED LIGHT, THEN BRASS, THEN A GENTLE GOLD, OR A SOFT AND QUIET AMETHYST..."
THE MAN STOPPED TALKING. THERE WAS A GLITTER IN HIS EYES THAT SCARED ME.
YOU KNOW WHAT AMETHYST IS?
I NODDED. MY CROTCH FELT UNCOMFORTABLE.
I DON'T KNOW HOW LONG IT WAS THAT I WAITED, IN MY ROOM. BUT TIME DIDN'T MEAN ANYTHING. NOT BACK THEN. WE HAD ALL THE TIME IN THE WORLD.

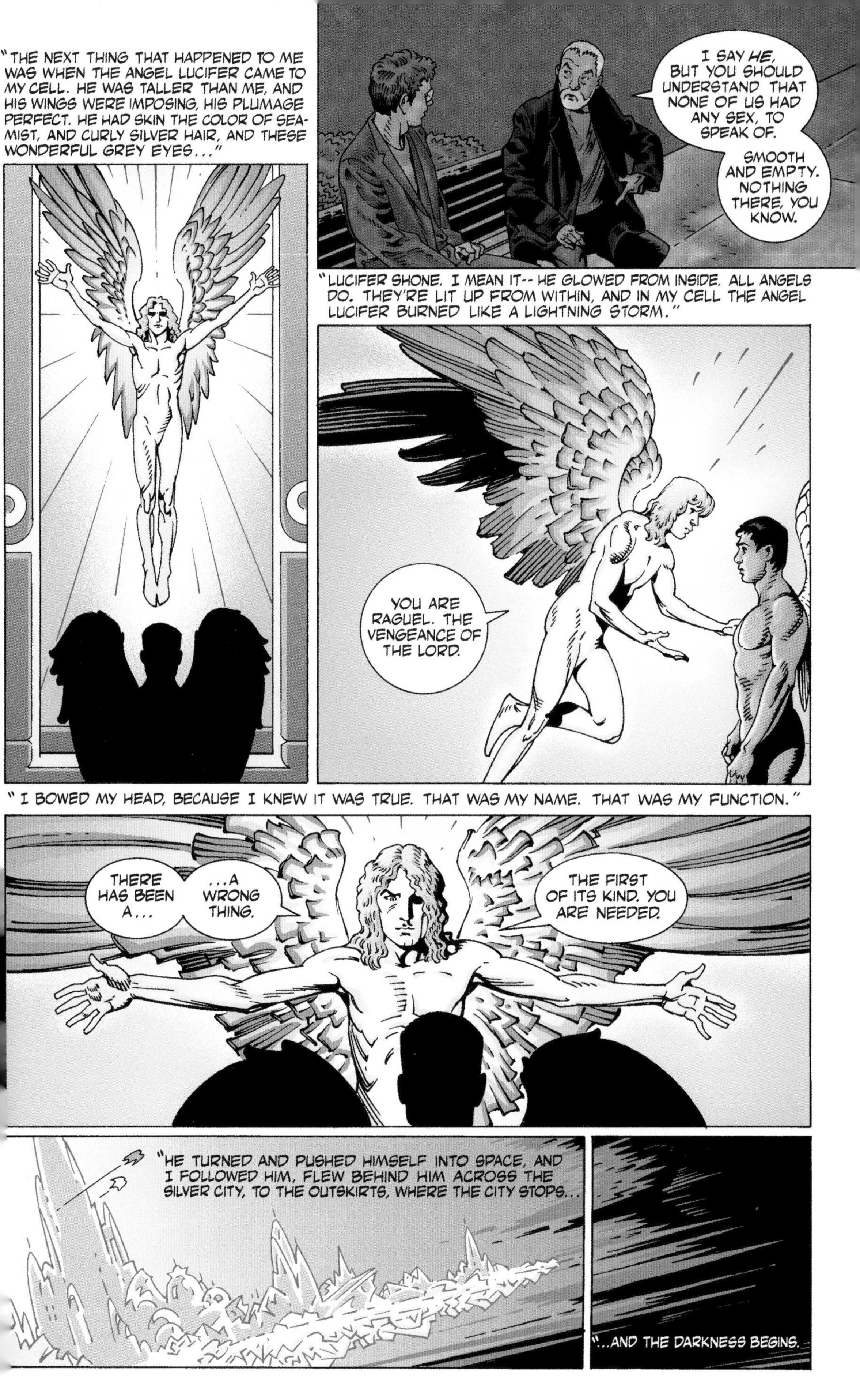
"THE NEXT THING THAT HAPPENED TO ME WAS WHEN THE ANGEL LUCIFER CAME TO MY CELL. HE WAS TALLER THAN ME, AND HIS WINGS WERE IMPOSING, HIS PLUMAGE PERFECT. HE HAD SKIN THE COLOR OF SEA-MIST, AND CURLY SILVER HAIR, AND THESE WONDERFUL GREY EYES..."
I SAY HE, BUT YOU SHOULD UNDERSTAND THAT NONE OF US HAD ANY SEX, TO SPEAK OF.
SMOOTH AND EMPTY. NOTHING THERE, YOU KNOW.
"LUCIFER SHONE. I MEAN IT-- HE GLOWED FROM INSIDE. ALL ANGELS DO. THEY'RE LIT UP FROM WITHIN, AND IN MY CELL THE ANGEL LUCIFER BURNED LIKE A LIGHTNING STORM."
YOU ARE RAGUEL. THE VENGEANCE OF THE LORD.
"I BOWED MY HEAD, BECAUSE I KNEW IT WAS TRUE. THAT WAS MY NAME. THAT WAS MY FUNCTION."
THERE HAS BEEN A...
...A WRONG THING.
THE FIRST OF ITS KIND. YOU ARE NEEDED.
"HE TURNED AND PUSHED HIMSELF INTO SPACE, AND I FOLLOWED HIM, FLEW BEHIND HIM ACROSS THE SILVER CITY, TO THE OUTSKIRTS, WHERE THE CITY STOPS...
"...AND THE DARKNESS BEGINS.

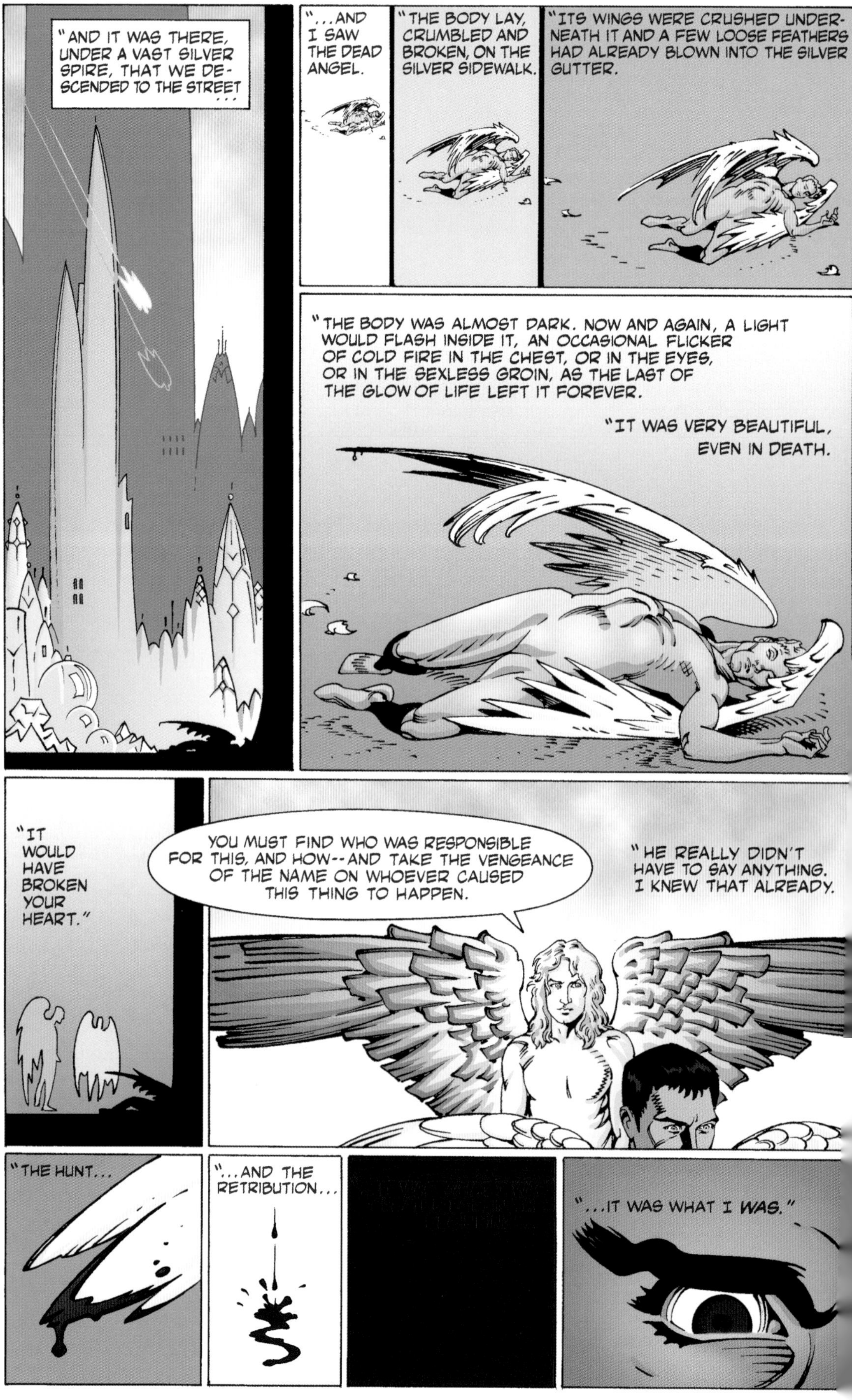
"AND IT WAS THERE, UNDER A VAST SILVER SPIRE, THAT WE DESCENDED TO THE STREET . . .
". . .AND I SAW THE DEAD ANGEL.
"THE BODY LAY, CRUMBLED AND BROKEN, ON THE SILVER SIDEWALK.
"ITS WINGS WERE CRUSHED UNDERNEATH IT AND A FEW LOOSE FEATHERS HAD ALREADY BLOWN INTO THE SILVER GUTTER.
"THE BODY WAS ALMOST DARK. NOW AND AGAIN, A LIGHT WOULD FLASH INSIDE IT, AN OCCASIONAL FLICKER OF COLD FIRE IN THE CHEST, OR IN THE EYES, OR IN THE SEXLESS GROIN, AS THE LAST OF THE GLOW OF LIFE LEFT IT FOREVER.
"IT WAS VERY BEAUTIFUL, EVEN IN DEATH.
"IT WOULD HAVE BROKEN YOUR HEART."
YOU MUST FIND WHO WAS RESPONSIBLE FOR THIS, AND HOW--AND TAKE THE VENGEANCE OF THE NAME ON WHOEVER CAUSED THIS THING TO HAPPEN.
"HE REALLY DIDN'T HAVE TO SAY ANYTHING. I KNEW THAT ALREADY.
"THE HUNT...
"...AND THE RETRIBUTION...
". . .IT WAS WHAT I *WAS*."

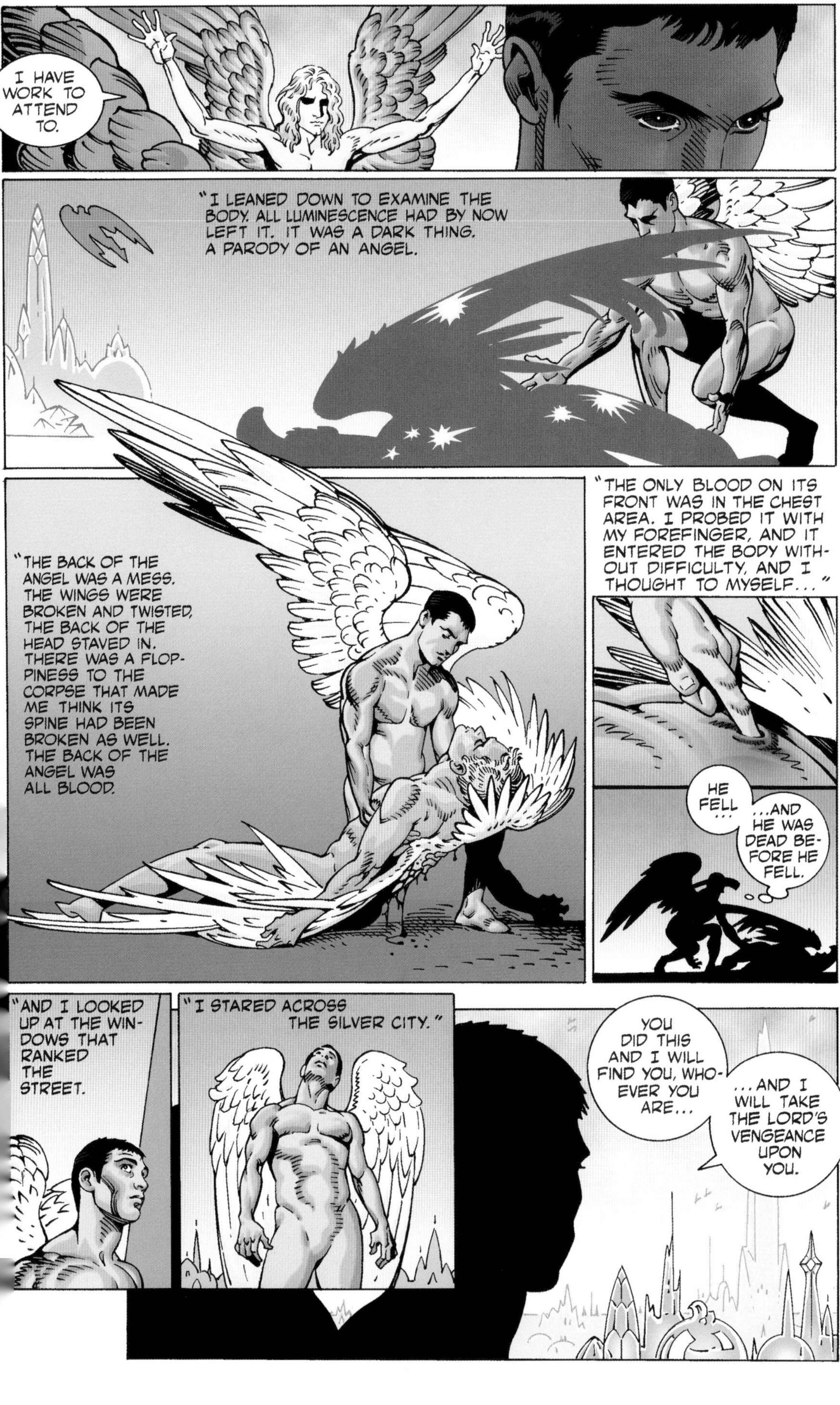
I HAVE WORK TO ATTEND TO.
"I LEANED DOWN TO EXAMINE THE BODY. ALL LUMINESCENCE HAD BY NOW LEFT IT. IT WAS A DARK THING. A PARODY OF AN ANGEL.
"THE BACK OF THE ANGEL WAS A MESS. THE WINGS WERE BROKEN AND TWISTED, THE BACK OF THE HEAD STAVED IN. THERE WAS A FLOPPINESS TO THE CORPSE THAT MADE ME THINK ITS SPINE HAD BEEN BROKEN AS WELL. THE BACK OF THE ANGEL WAS ALL BLOOD.
"THE ONLY BLOOD ON ITS FRONT WAS IN THE CHEST AREA. I PROBED IT WITH MY FOREFINGER, AND IT ENTERED THE BODY WITHOUT DIFFICULTY, AND I THOUGHT TO MYSELF..."
HE FELL...
...AND HE WAS DEAD BEFORE HE FELL.
"AND I LOOKED UP AT THE WINDOWS THAT RANKED THE STREET.
"I STARED ACROSS THE SILVER CITY."
YOU DID THIS AND I WILL FIND YOU, WHOEVER YOU ARE...
...AND I WILL TAKE THE LORD'S VENGEANCE UPON YOU.

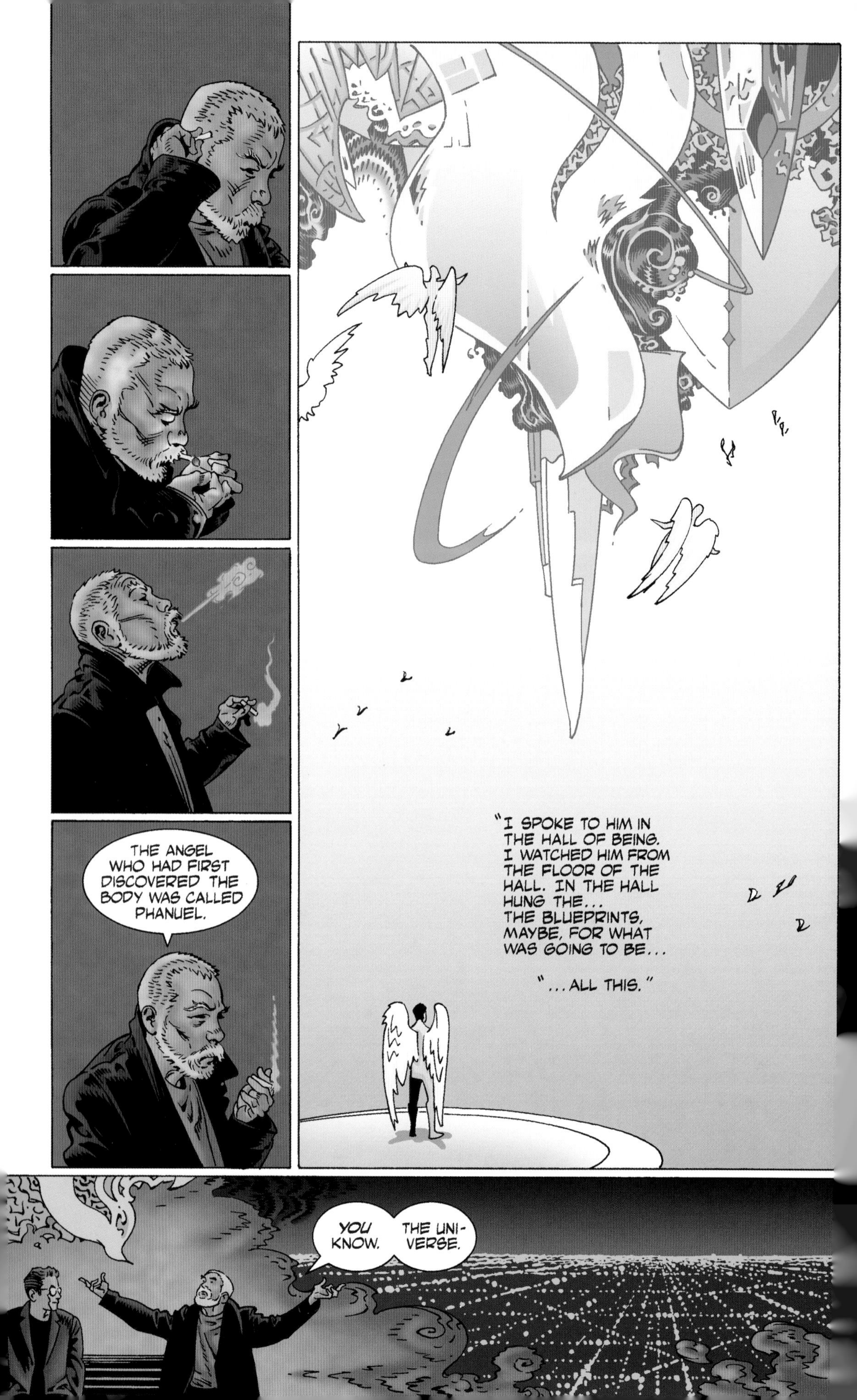

THE ANGEL WHO HAD FIRST DISCOVERED THE BODY WAS CALLED PHANUEL.
"I SPOKE TO HIM IN THE HALL OF BEING. I WATCHED HIM FROM THE FLOOR OF THE HALL. IN THE HALL HUNG THE... THE BLUEPRINTS, MAYBE, FOR WHAT WAS GOING TO BE...
"...ALL THIS."
YOU KNOW.
THE UNI-VERSE.

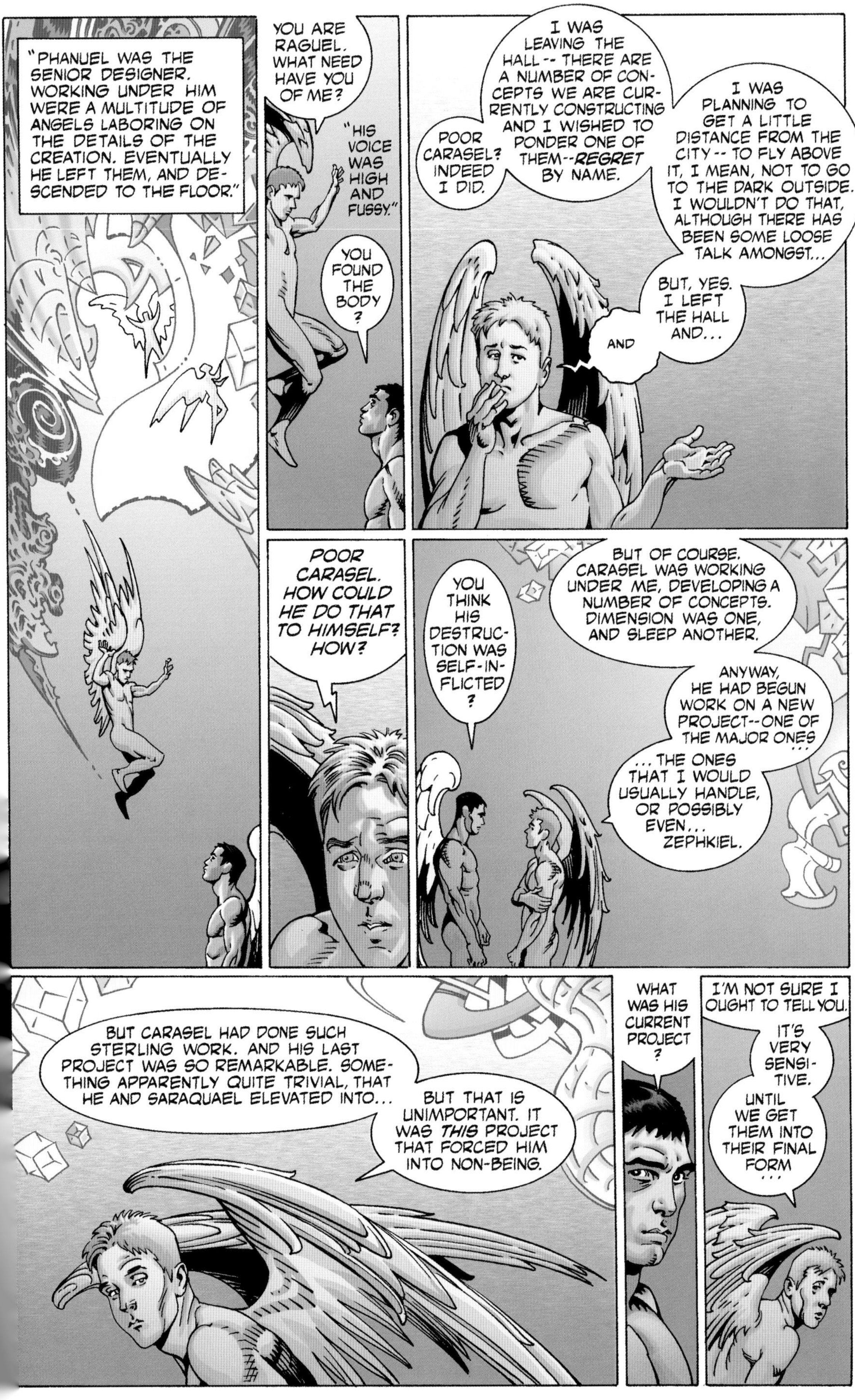
"PHANUEL WAS THE SENIOR DESIGNER. WORKING UNDER HIM WERE A MULTITUDE OF ANGELS LABORING ON THE DETAILS OF THE CREATION. EVENTUALLY HE LEFT THEM, AND DESCENDED TO THE FLOOR."
YOU ARE RAGUEL. WHAT NEED HAVE YOU OF ME?
"HIS VOICE WAS HIGH AND FUSSY."
YOU FOUND THE BODY?
POOR CARASEL? INDEED I DID.
I WAS LEAVING THE HALL -- THERE ARE A NUMBER OF CONCEPTS WE ARE CURRENTLY CONSTRUCTING AND I WISHED TO PONDER ONE OF THEM--*REGRET* BY NAME.
I WAS PLANNING TO GET A LITTLE DISTANCE FROM THE CITY -- TO FLY ABOVE IT, I MEAN, NOT TO GO TO THE DARK OUTSIDE. I WOULDN'T DO THAT, ALTHOUGH THERE HAS BEEN SOME LOOSE TALK AMONGST...
BUT, YES. I LEFT THE HALL AND...
AND
POOR CARASEL. HOW COULD HE DO THAT TO HIMSELF? HOW?
YOU THINK HIS DESTRUCTION WAS SELF-INFLICTED?
BUT OF COURSE. CARASEL WAS WORKING UNDER ME, DEVELOPING A NUMBER OF CONCEPTS. DIMENSION WAS ONE, AND SLEEP ANOTHER.
ANYWAY, HE HAD BEGUN WORK ON A NEW PROJECT--ONE OF THE MAJOR ONES...
...THE ONES THAT I WOULD USUALLY HANDLE, OR POSSIBLY EVEN... ZEPHKIEL.
BUT CARASEL HAD DONE SUCH STERLING WORK. AND HIS LAST PROJECT WAS SO REMARKABLE. SOMETHING APPARENTLY QUITE TRIVIAL, THAT HE AND SARAQUAEL ELEVATED INTO...
BUT THAT IS UNIMPORTANT. IT WAS *THIS* PROJECT THAT FORCED HIM INTO NON-BEING.
WHAT WAS HIS CURRENT PROJECT?
I'M NOT SURE I OUGHT TO TELL YOU.
IT'S VERY SENSITIVE.
UNTIL WE GET THEM INTO THEIR FINAL FORM...

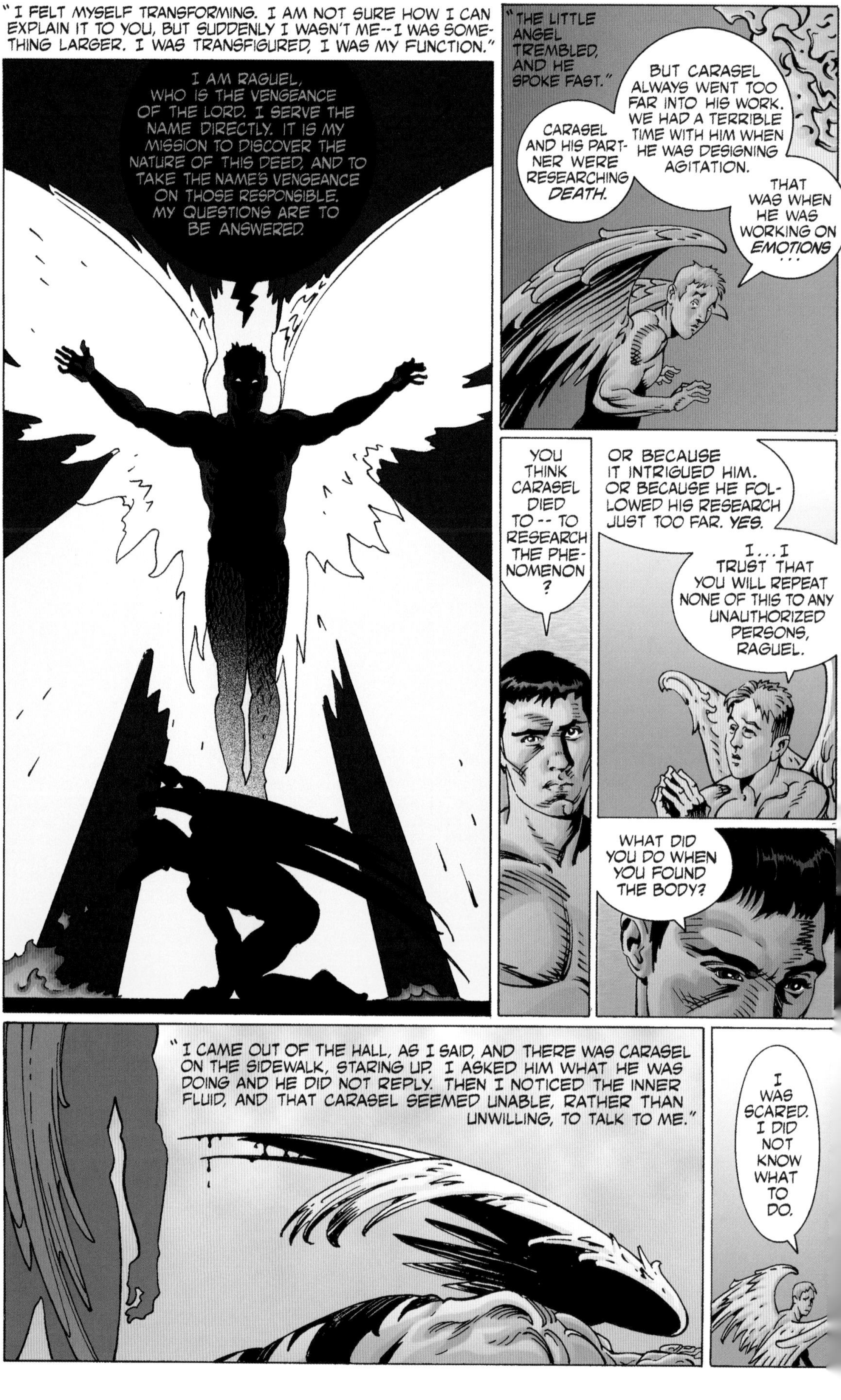
"I FELT MYSELF TRANSFORMING. I AM NOT SURE HOW I CAN EXPLAIN IT TO YOU, BUT SUDDENLY I WASN'T ME--I WAS SOMETHING LARGER. I WAS TRANSFIGURED, I WAS MY FUNCTION."
I AM RAGUEL, WHO IS THE VENGEANCE OF THE LORD. I SERVE THE NAME DIRECTLY. IT IS MY MISSION TO DISCOVER THE NATURE OF THIS DEED, AND TO TAKE THE NAME'S VENGEANCE ON THOSE RESPONSIBLE. MY QUESTIONS ARE TO BE ANSWERED.
"THE LITTLE ANGEL TREMBLED, AND HE SPOKE FAST."
CARASEL AND HIS PARTNER WERE RESEARCHING *DEATH*.
BUT CARASEL ALWAYS WENT TOO FAR INTO HIS WORK. WE HAD A TERRIBLE TIME WITH HIM WHEN HE WAS DESIGNING AGITATION.
THAT WAS WHEN HE WAS WORKING ON *EMOTIONS* . . .
YOU THINK CARASEL DIED TO -- TO RESEARCH THE PHENOMENON?
OR BECAUSE IT INTRIGUED HIM. OR BECAUSE HE FOLLOWED HIS RESEARCH JUST TOO FAR. *YES.*
I . . . I TRUST THAT YOU WILL REPEAT NONE OF THIS TO ANY UNAUTHORIZED PERSONS, RAGUEL.
WHAT DID YOU DO WHEN YOU FOUND THE BODY?
"I CAME OUT OF THE HALL, AS I SAID, AND THERE WAS CARASEL ON THE SIDEWALK, STARING UP. I ASKED HIM WHAT HE WAS DOING AND HE DID NOT REPLY. THEN I NOTICED THE INNER FLUID, AND THAT CARASEL SEEMED UNABLE, RATHER THAN UNWILLING, TO TALK TO ME."
I WAS SCARED. I DID NOT KNOW WHAT TO DO.

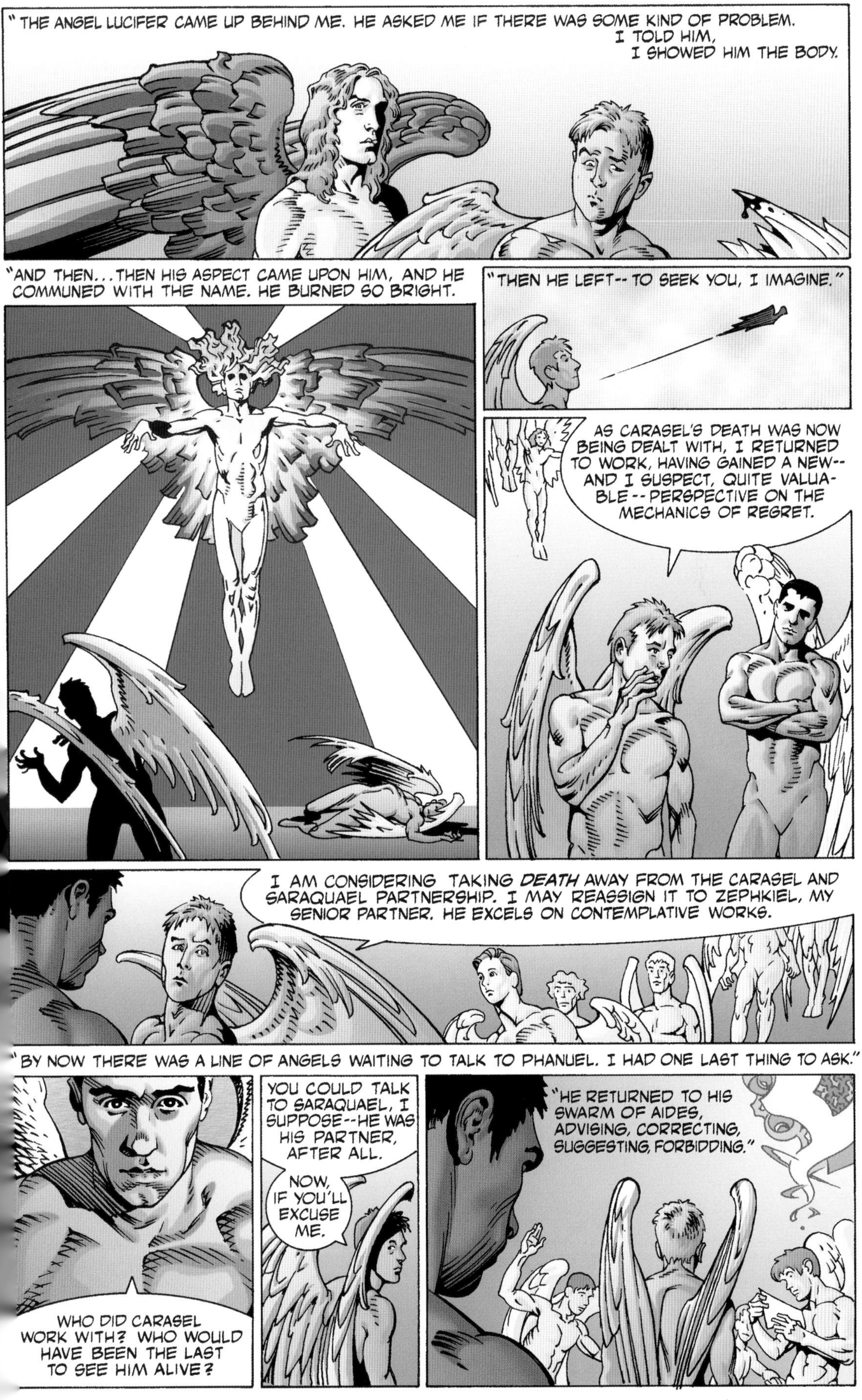
"THE ANGEL LUCIFER CAME UP BEHIND ME. HE ASKED ME IF THERE WAS SOME KIND OF PROBLEM.
I TOLD HIM,
I SHOWED HIM THE BODY.
"AND THEN...THEN HIS ASPECT CAME UPON HIM, AND HE COMMUNED WITH THE NAME. HE BURNED SO BRIGHT.
"THEN HE LEFT-- TO SEEK YOU, I IMAGINE."
AS CARASEL'S DEATH WAS NOW BEING DEALT WITH, I RETURNED TO WORK, HAVING GAINED A NEW-- AND I SUSPECT, QUITE VALUABLE--PERSPECTIVE ON THE MECHANICS OF REGRET.
I AM CONSIDERING TAKING DEATH AWAY FROM THE CARASEL AND SARAQUAEL PARTNERSHIP. I MAY REASSIGN IT TO ZEPHKIEL, MY SENIOR PARTNER. HE EXCELS ON CONTEMPLATIVE WORKS.
"BY NOW THERE WAS A LINE OF ANGELS WAITING TO TALK TO PHANUEL. I HAD ONE LAST THING TO ASK."
WHO DID CARASEL WORK WITH? WHO WOULD HAVE BEEN THE LAST TO SEE HIM ALIVE?
YOU COULD TALK TO SARAQUAEL, I SUPPOSE--HE WAS HIS PARTNER, AFTER ALL.
NOW, IF YOU'LL EXCUSE ME.
"HE RETURNED TO HIS SWARM OF AIDES, ADVISING, CORRECTING, SUGGESTING, FORBIDDING."

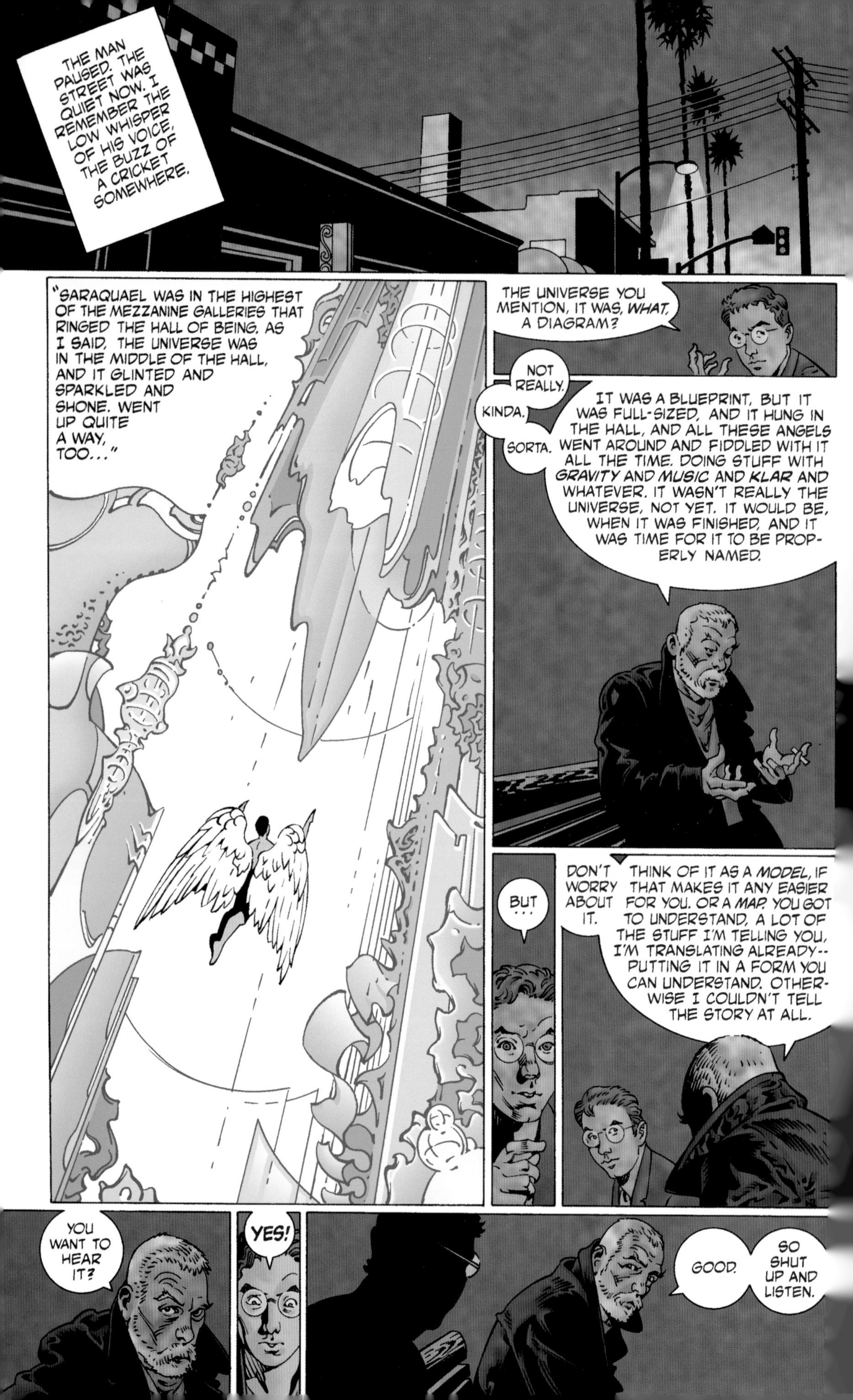
THE MAN PAUSED. THE STREET WAS QUIET NOW. I REMEMBER THE LOW WHISPER OF HIS VOICE, THE BUZZ OF A CRICKET SOMEWHERE.
"SARAQUAEL WAS IN THE HIGHEST OF THE MEZZANINE GALLERIES THAT RINGED THE HALL OF BEING. AS I SAID, THE UNIVERSE WAS IN THE MIDDLE OF THE HALL, AND IT GLINTED AND SPARKLED AND SHONE. WENT UP QUITE A WAY, TOO..."
THE UNIVERSE YOU MENTION, IT WAS, WHAT, A DIAGRAM?
NOT REALLY.
KINDA.
SORTA.
IT WAS A BLUEPRINT, BUT IT WAS FULL-SIZED, AND IT HUNG IN THE HALL, AND ALL THESE ANGELS WENT AROUND AND FIDDLED WITH IT ALL THE TIME. DOING STUFF WITH GRAVITY AND MUSIC AND KLAR AND WHATEVER. IT WASN'T REALLY THE UNIVERSE, NOT YET. IT WOULD BE, WHEN IT WAS FINISHED, AND IT WAS TIME FOR IT TO BE PROPERLY NAMED.
BUT...
DON'T WORRY ABOUT IT.
THINK OF IT AS A MODEL, IF THAT MAKES IT ANY EASIER FOR YOU. OR A MAP. YOU GOT TO UNDERSTAND, A LOT OF THE STUFF I'M TELLING YOU, I'M TRANSLATING ALREADY-- PUTTING IT IN A FORM YOU CAN UNDERSTAND. OTHERWISE I COULDN'T TELL THE STORY AT ALL.
YOU WANT TO HEAR IT?
YES!
GOOD.
SO SHUT UP AND LISTEN.

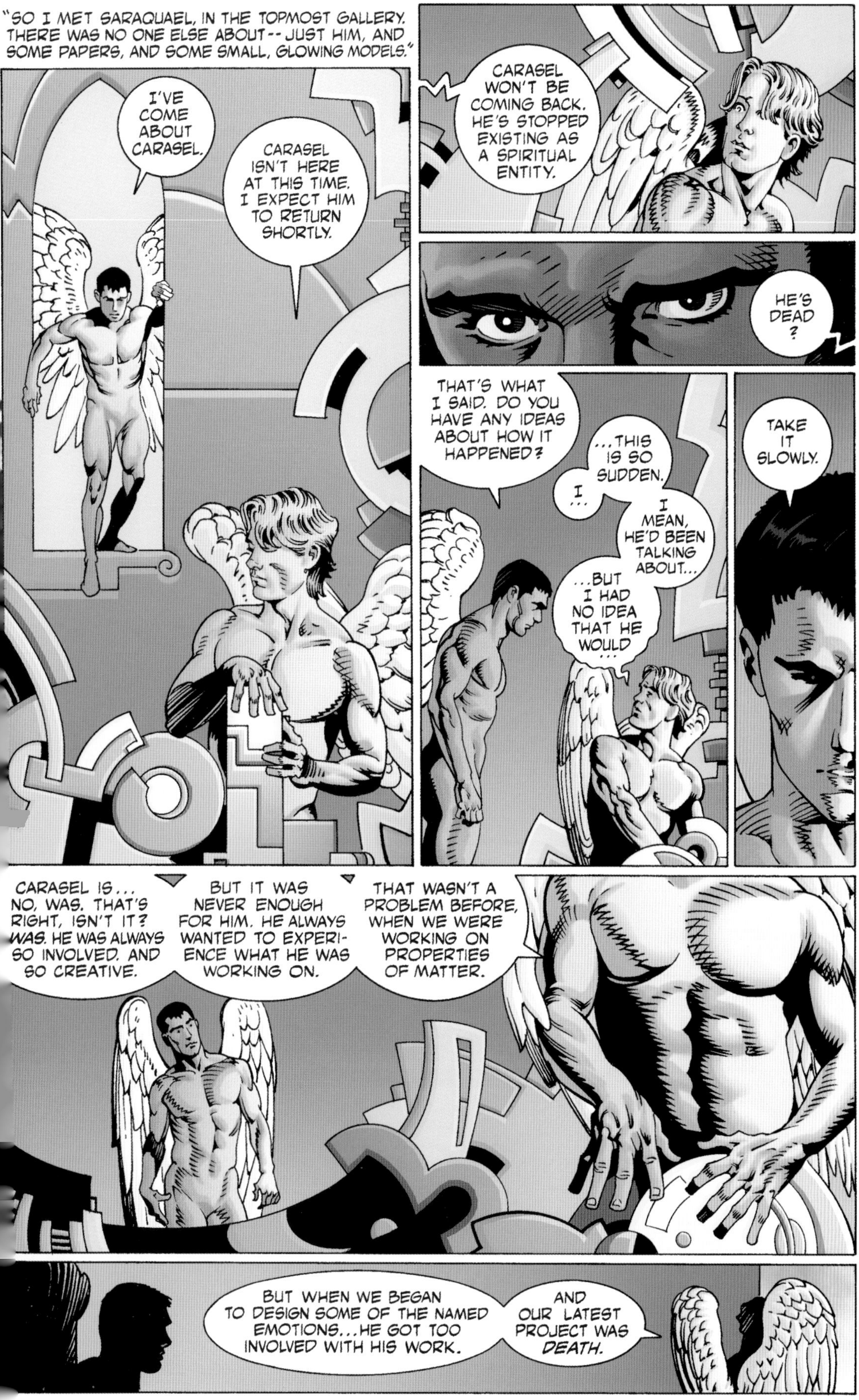
"SO I MET SARAQUAEL, IN THE TOPMOST GALLERY. THERE WAS NO ONE ELSE ABOUT -- JUST HIM, AND SOME PAPERS, AND SOME SMALL, GLOWING MODELS."
I'VE COME ABOUT CARASEL.
CARASEL ISN'T HERE AT THIS TIME. I EXPECT HIM TO RETURN SHORTLY.
CARASEL WON'T BE COMING BACK. HE'S STOPPED EXISTING AS A SPIRITUAL ENTITY.
HE'S DEAD?
THAT'S WHAT I SAID. DO YOU HAVE ANY IDEAS ABOUT HOW IT HAPPENED?
I...
...THIS IS SO SUDDEN.
I MEAN, HE'D BEEN TALKING ABOUT...
...BUT I HAD NO IDEA THAT HE WOULD...
TAKE IT SLOWLY.
CARASEL IS... NO, WAS. THAT'S RIGHT, ISN'T IT? *WAS*. HE WAS ALWAYS SO INVOLVED. AND SO CREATIVE.
BUT IT WAS NEVER ENOUGH FOR HIM. HE ALWAYS WANTED TO EXPERI-ENCE WHAT HE WAS WORKING ON.
THAT WASN'T A PROBLEM BEFORE, WHEN WE WERE WORKING ON PROPERTIES OF MATTER.
BUT WHEN WE BEGAN TO DESIGN SOME OF THE NAMED EMOTIONS...HE GOT TOO INVOLVED WITH HIS WORK.
AND OUR LATEST PROJECT WAS *DEATH*.

"HE STOOD UP AND WALKED TO THE WINDOW. THERE WAS NO VIEW OF THE SILVER CITY FROM HIS WINDOW--JUST A REFLECTED GLOW FROM THE CITY AND THE SKY BEHIND US, HANGING IN THE AIR, AND BEYOND THAT, THE DARK."

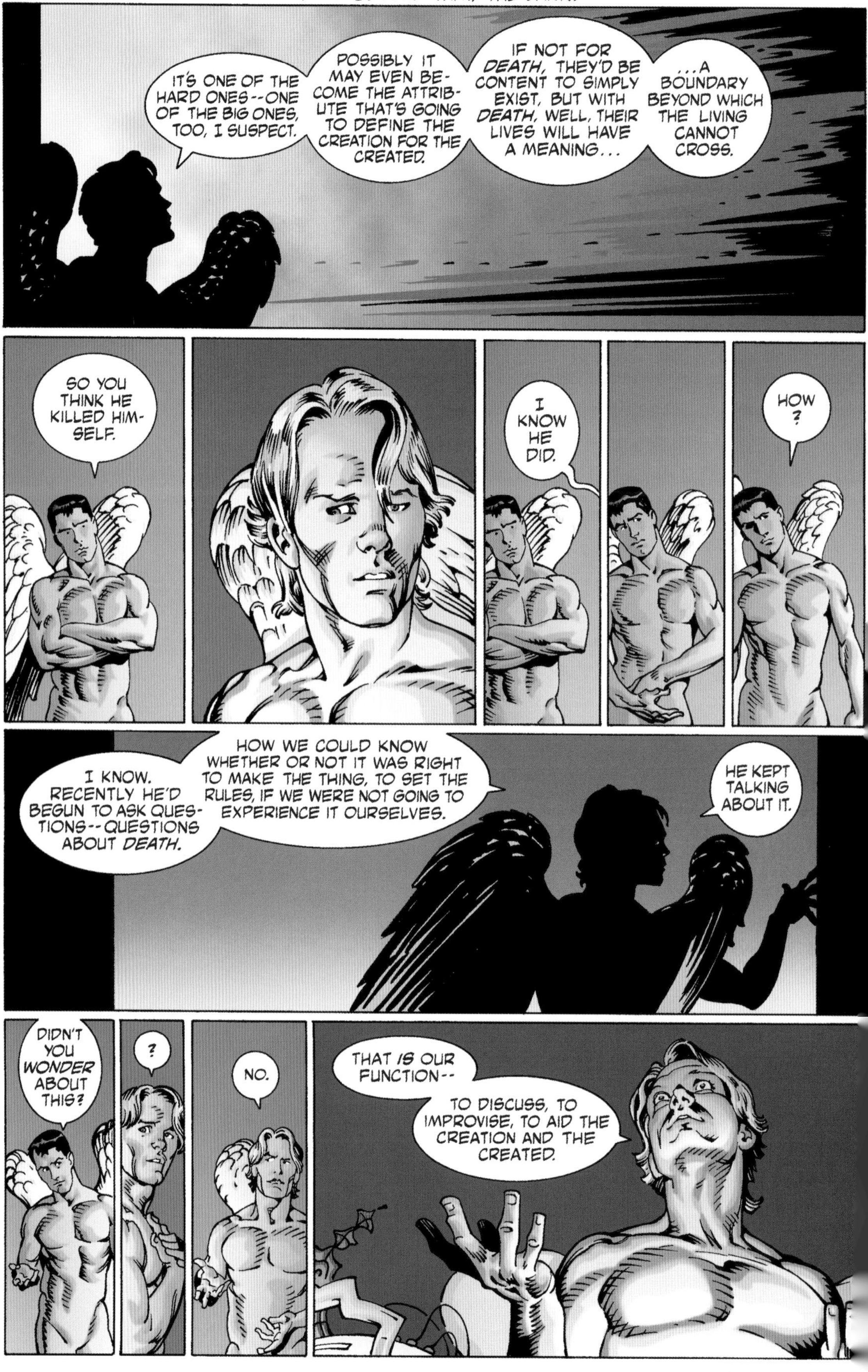
IT'S ONE OF THE HARD ONES--ONE OF THE BIG ONES, TOO, I SUSPECT.
POSSIBLY IT MAY EVEN BECOME THE ATTRIBUTE THAT'S GOING TO DEFINE THE CREATION FOR THE CREATED.
IF NOT FOR *DEATH*, THEY'D BE CONTENT TO SIMPLY EXIST, BUT WITH *DEATH*, WELL, THEIR LIVES WILL HAVE A MEANING...
...A BOUNDARY BEYOND WHICH THE LIVING CANNOT CROSS.
SO YOU THINK HE KILLED HIMSELF.
I KNOW HE DID.
HOW?
I KNOW. RECENTLY HE'D BEGUN TO ASK QUESTIONS--QUESTIONS ABOUT *DEATH*.
HOW WE COULD KNOW WHETHER OR NOT IT WAS RIGHT TO MAKE THE THING, TO SET THE RULES, IF WE WERE NOT GOING TO EXPERIENCE IT OURSELVES.
HE KEPT TALKING ABOUT IT.
DIDN'T YOU *WONDER* ABOUT THIS?
?
NO.
THAT *IS* OUR FUNCTION--
TO DISCUSS, TO IMPROVISE, TO AID THE CREATION AND THE CREATED.

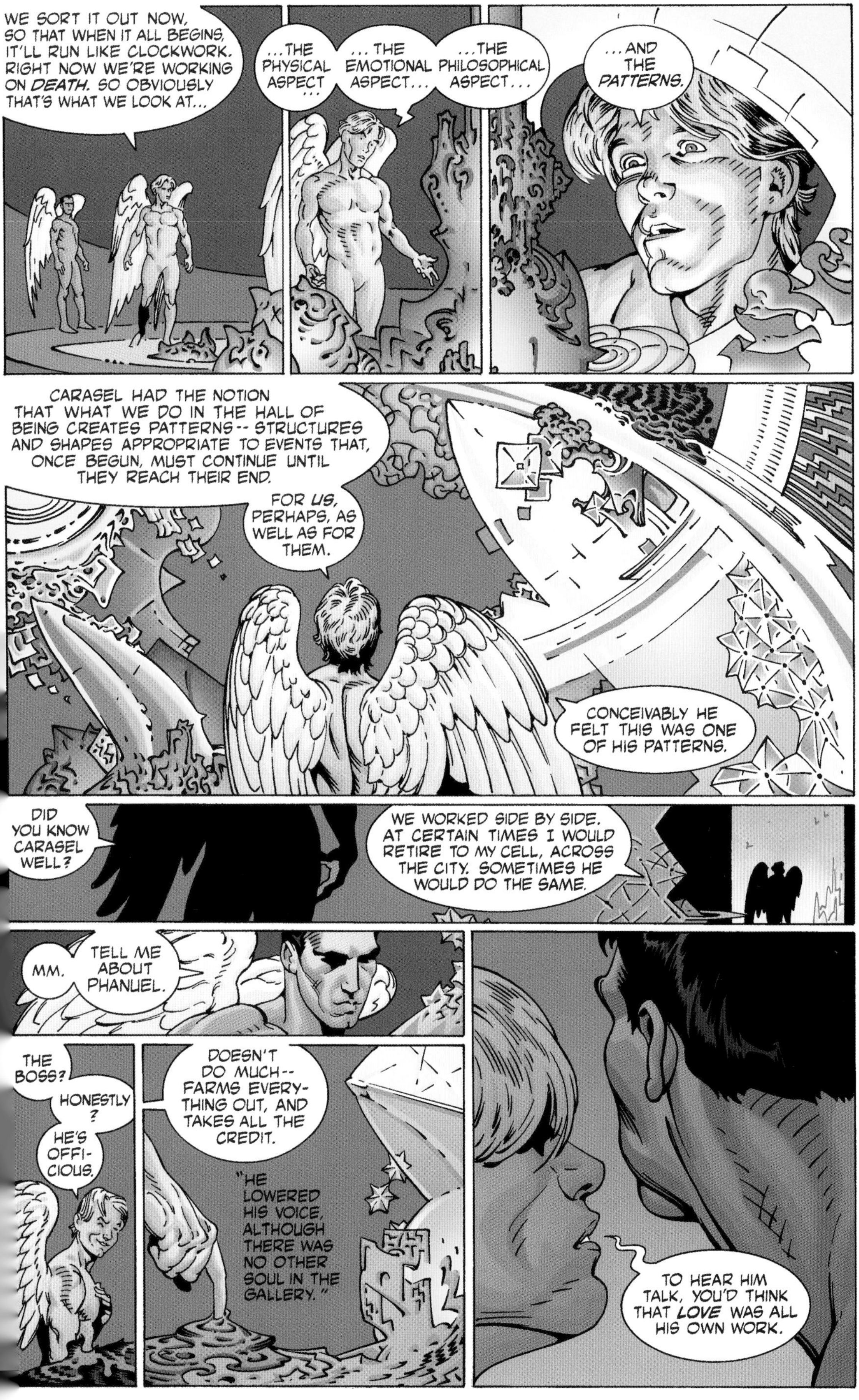
WE SORT IT OUT NOW, SO THAT WHEN IT ALL BEGINS, IT'LL RUN LIKE CLOCKWORK. RIGHT NOW WE'RE WORKING ON *DEATH.* SO OBVIOUSLY THAT'S WHAT WE LOOK AT...
...THE PHYSICAL ASPECT...
...THE EMOTIONAL ASPECT...
...THE PHILOSOPHICAL ASPECT...
...AND THE *PATTERNS.*
CARASEL HAD THE NOTION THAT WHAT WE DO IN THE HALL OF BEING CREATES PATTERNS-- STRUCTURES AND SHAPES APPROPRIATE TO EVENTS THAT, ONCE BEGUN, MUST CONTINUE UNTIL THEY REACH THEIR END.
FOR *US,* PERHAPS, AS WELL AS FOR THEM.
CONCEIVABLY HE FELT THIS WAS ONE OF HIS PATTERNS.
DID YOU KNOW CARASEL WELL?
WE WORKED SIDE BY SIDE. AT CERTAIN TIMES I WOULD RETIRE TO MY CELL, ACROSS THE CITY. SOMETIMES HE WOULD DO THE SAME.
MM.
TELL ME ABOUT PHANUEL.
THE BOSS?
HONESTLY?
HE'S OFFICIOUS.
DOESN'T DO MUCH-- FARMS EVERYTHING OUT, AND TAKES ALL THE CREDIT.
"HE LOWERED HIS VOICE, ALTHOUGH THERE WAS NO OTHER SOUL IN THE GALLERY."
TO HEAR HIM TALK, YOU'D THINK THAT *LOVE* WAS ALL HIS OWN WORK.

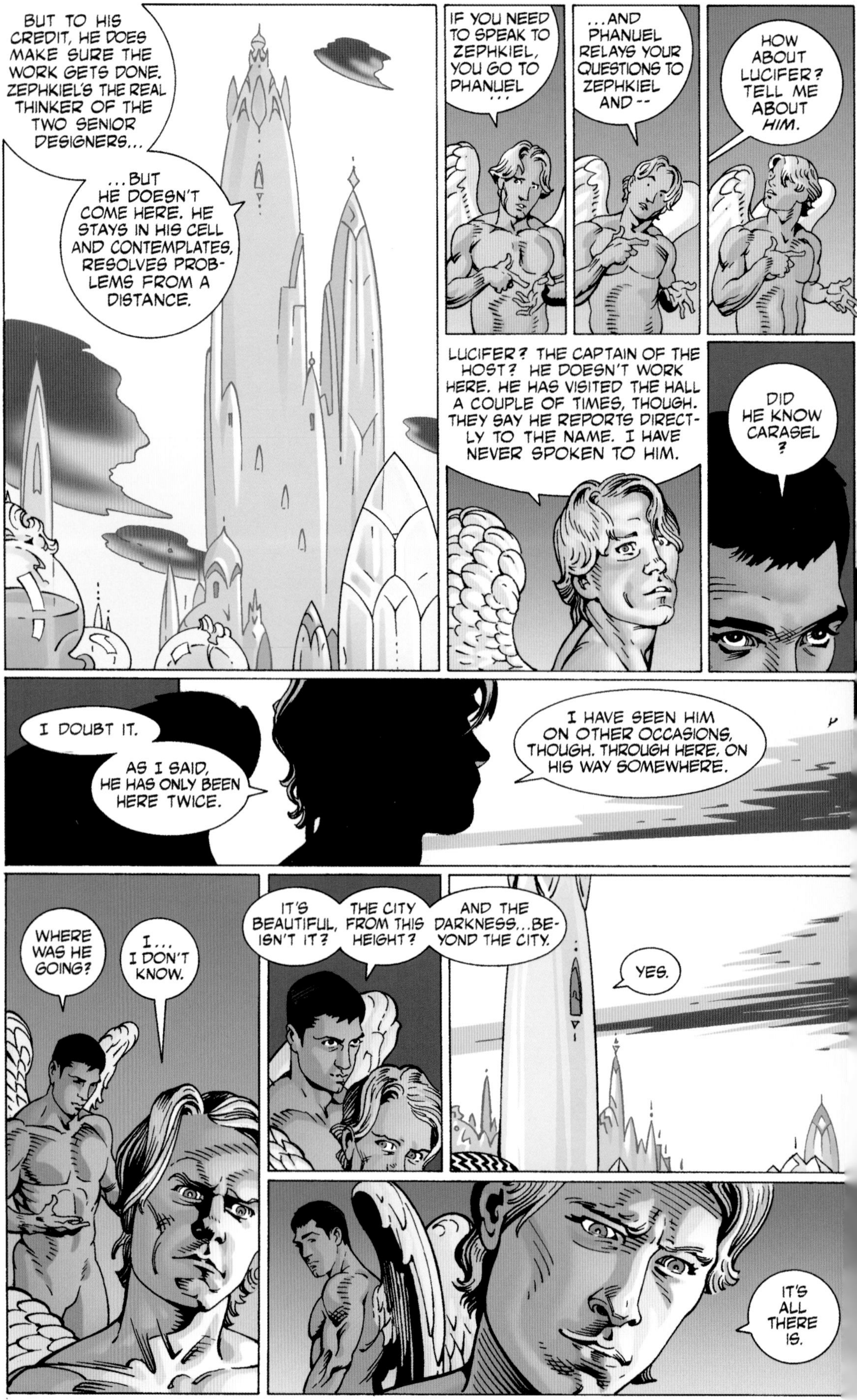
BUT TO HIS CREDIT, HE DOES MAKE SURE THE WORK GETS DONE. ZEPHKIEL'S THE REAL THINKER OF THE TWO SENIOR DESIGNERS...
...BUT HE DOESN'T COME HERE. HE STAYS IN HIS CELL AND CONTEMPLATES, RESOLVES PROB-LEMS FROM A DISTANCE.
IF YOU NEED TO SPEAK TO ZEPHKIEL, YOU GO TO PHANUEL...
...AND PHANUEL RELAYS YOUR QUESTIONS TO ZEPHKIEL AND --
HOW ABOUT LUCIFER? TELL ME ABOUT *HIM*.
LUCIFER? THE CAPTAIN OF THE HOST? HE DOESN'T WORK HERE. HE HAS VISITED THE HALL A COUPLE OF TIMES, THOUGH. THEY SAY HE REPORTS DIRECT-LY TO THE NAME. I HAVE NEVER SPOKEN TO HIM.
DID HE KNOW CARASEL?
I DOUBT IT.
AS I SAID, HE HAS ONLY BEEN HERE TWICE.
I HAVE SEEN HIM ON OTHER OCCASIONS, THOUGH. THROUGH HERE, ON HIS WAY SOMEWHERE.
WHERE WAS HE GOING?
I... I DON'T KNOW.
IT'S BEAUTIFUL, ISN'T IT?
THE CITY FROM THIS HEIGHT?
AND THE DARKNESS...BE-YOND THE CITY.
YES.
IT'S ALL THERE IS.

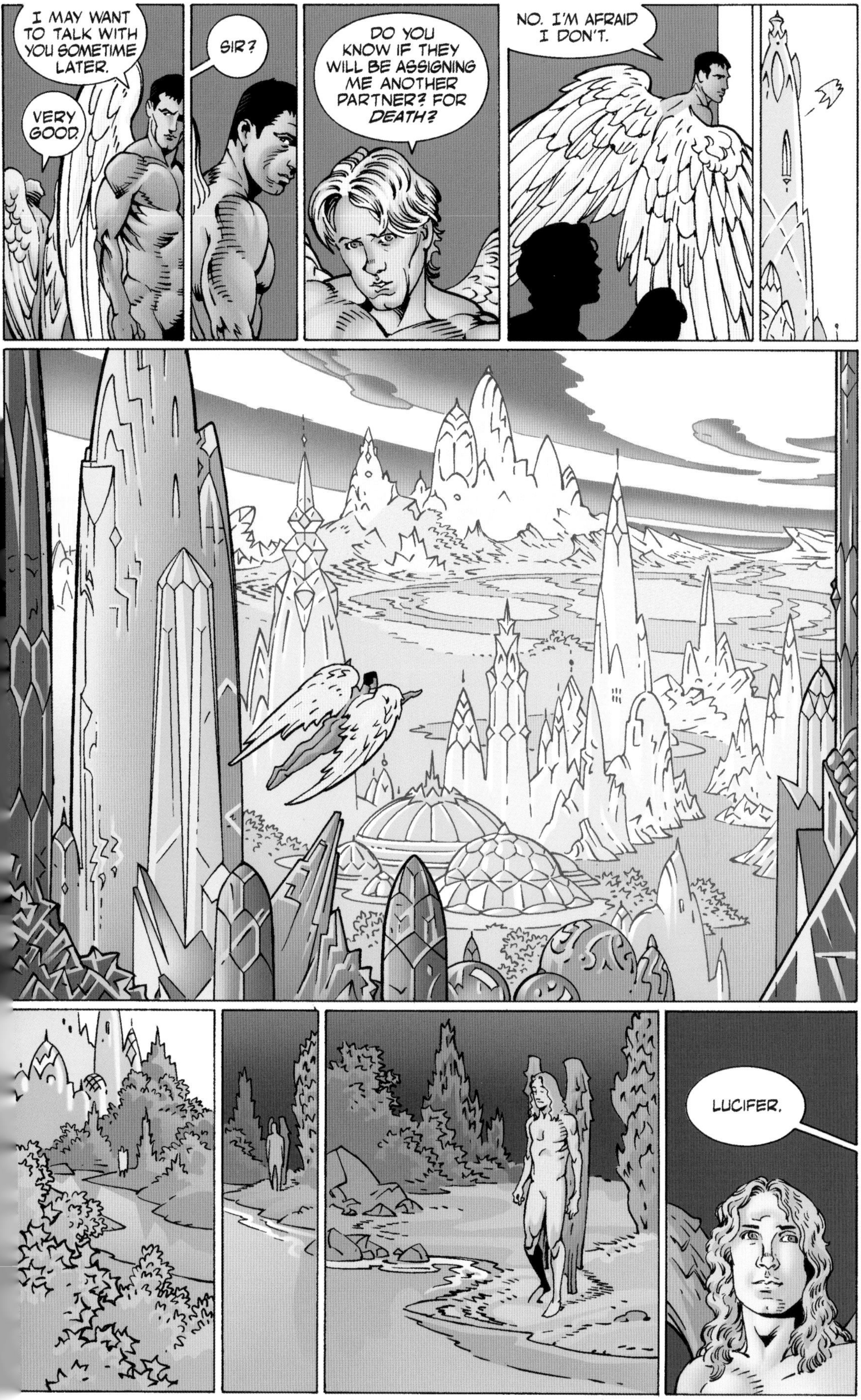
I MAY WANT TO TALK WITH YOU SOMETIME LATER.
VERY GOOD.
SIR?
DO YOU KNOW IF THEY WILL BE ASSIGNING ME ANOTHER PARTNER? FOR *DEATH*?
NO. I'M AFRAID I DON'T.
LUCIFER.

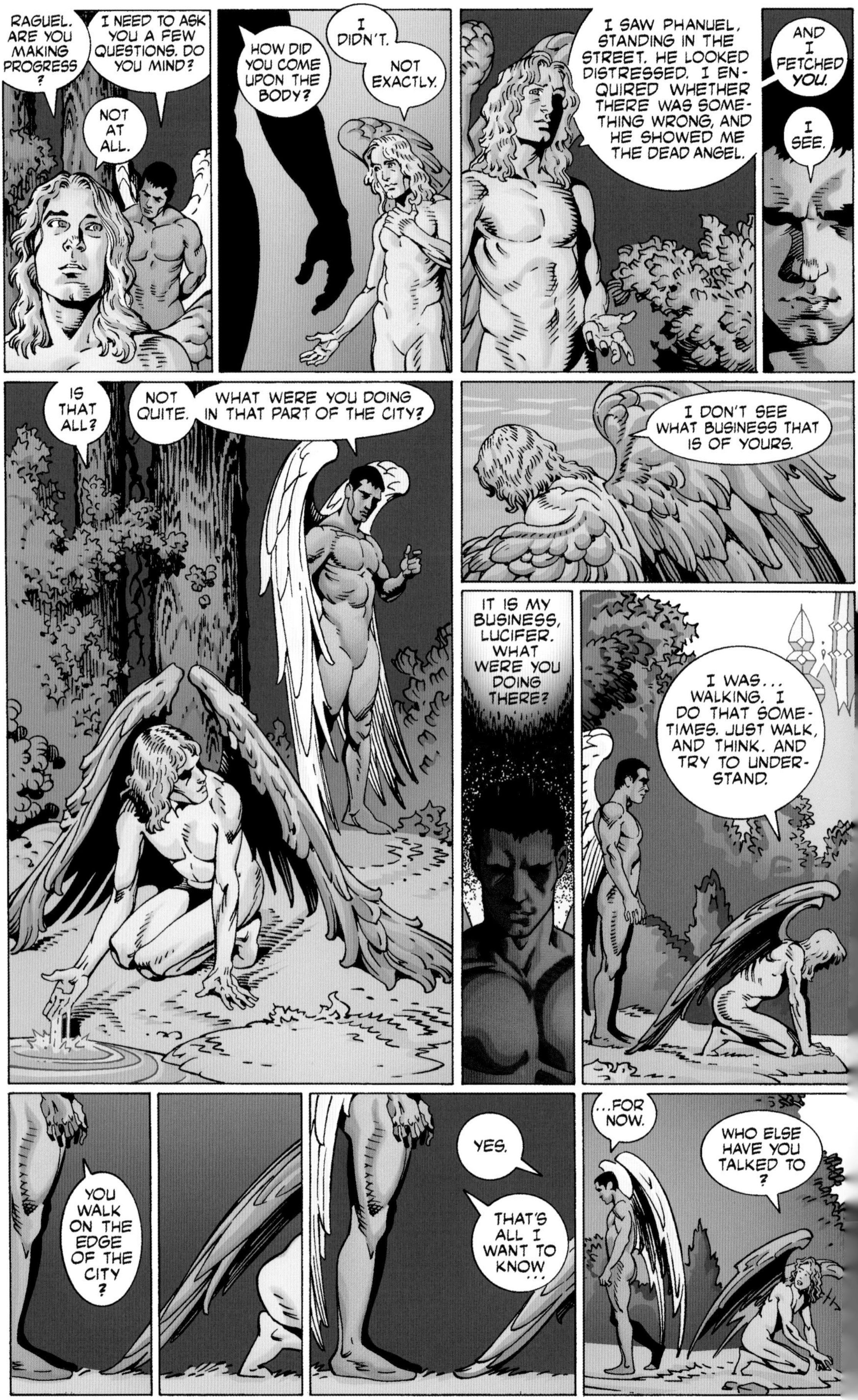

RAGUEL. ARE YOU MAKING PROGRESS?
I NEED TO ASK YOU A FEW QUESTIONS. DO YOU MIND?
NOT AT ALL.
HOW DID YOU COME UPON THE BODY?
I DIDN'T.
NOT EXACTLY.
I SAW PHANUEL, STANDING IN THE STREET. HE LOOKED DISTRESSED. I ENQUIRED WHETHER THERE WAS SOMETHING WRONG, AND HE SHOWED ME THE DEAD ANGEL.
AND I FETCHED YOU.
I SEE.
IS THAT ALL?
NOT QUITE.
WHAT WERE YOU DOING IN THAT PART OF THE CITY?
I DON'T SEE WHAT BUSINESS THAT IS OF YOURS.
IT IS MY BUSINESS, LUCIFER. WHAT WERE YOU DOING THERE?
I WAS... WALKING. I DO THAT SOMETIMES. JUST WALK, AND THINK. AND TRY TO UNDERSTAND.
YOU WALK ON THE EDGE OF THE CITY?
YES.
THAT'S ALL I WANT TO KNOW...
...FOR NOW.
WHO ELSE HAVE YOU TALKED TO?

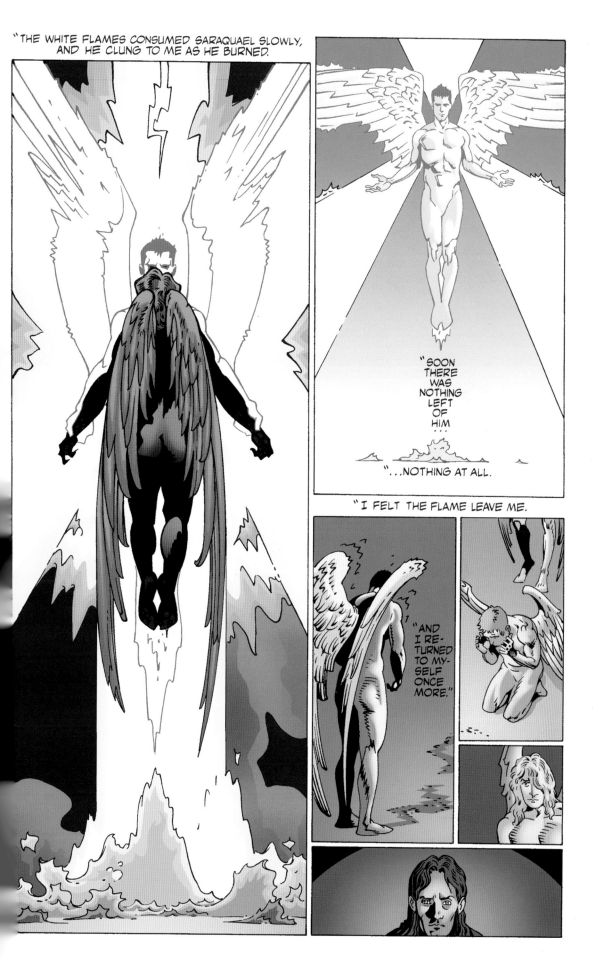

"THE WHITE FLAMES CONSUMED SARAQUAEL SLOWLY, AND HE CLUNG TO ME AS HE BURNED.

"SOON THERE WAS NOTHING LEFT OF HIM...

"...NOTHING AT ALL.

"I FELT THE FLAME LEAVE ME.

"AND I RETURNED TO MYSELF ONCE MORE."

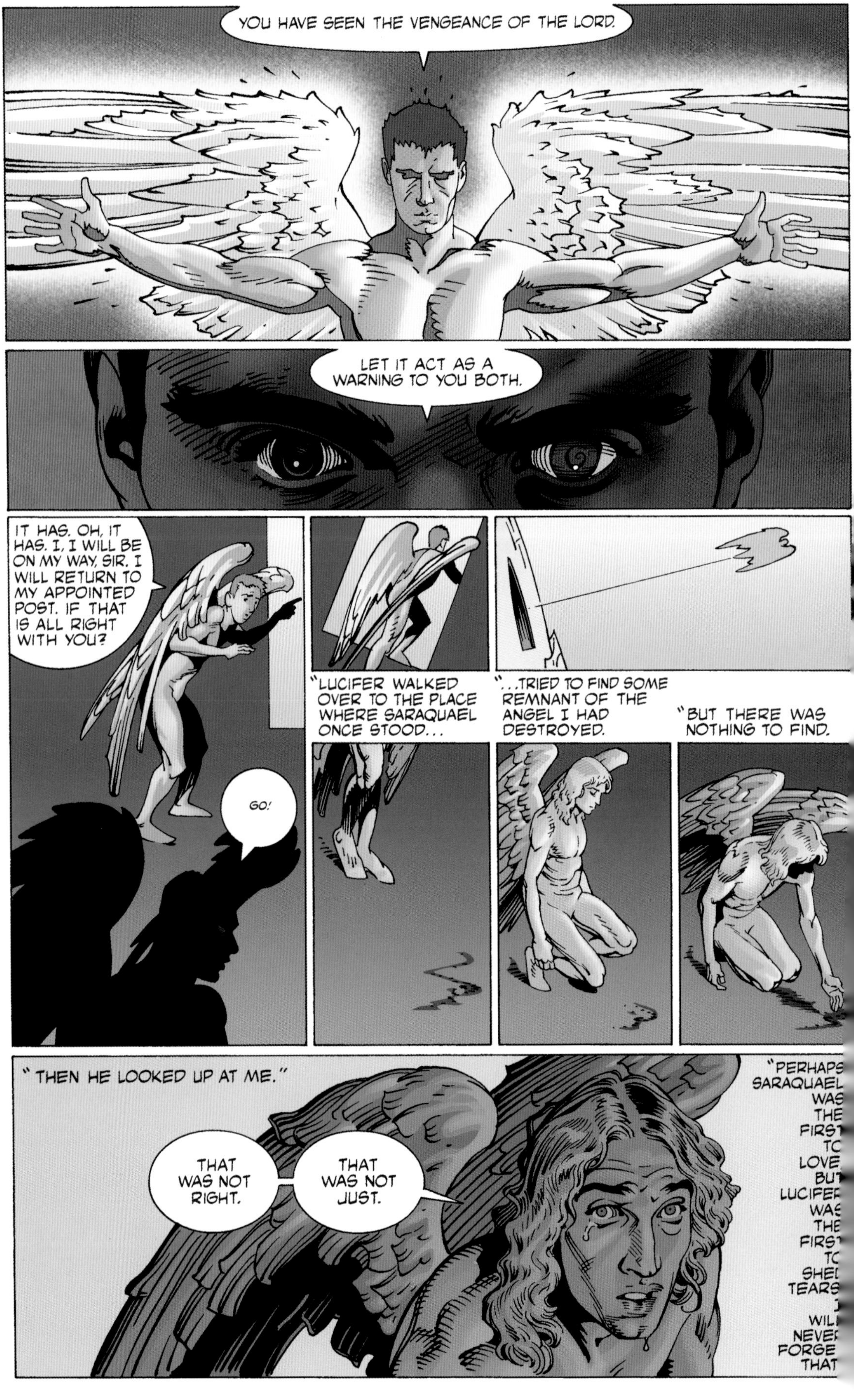
YOU HAVE SEEN THE VENGEANCE OF THE LORD.
LET IT ACT AS A WARNING TO YOU BOTH.
IT HAS. OH, IT HAS. I, I WILL BE ON MY WAY, SIR. I WILL RETURN TO MY APPOINTED POST. IF THAT IS ALL RIGHT WITH YOU?
GO!
"LUCIFER WALKED OVER TO THE PLACE WHERE SARAQUAEL ONCE STOOD...
"...TRIED TO FIND SOME REMNANT OF THE ANGEL I HAD DESTROYED.
"BUT THERE WAS NOTHING TO FIND.
"THEN HE LOOKED UP AT ME."
THAT WAS NOT RIGHT.
THAT WAS NOT JUST.
"PERHAPS SARAQUAEL WAS THE FIRST TO LOVE, BUT LUCIFER WAS THE FIRST TO SHED TEARS. WILL NEVER FORGE THAT

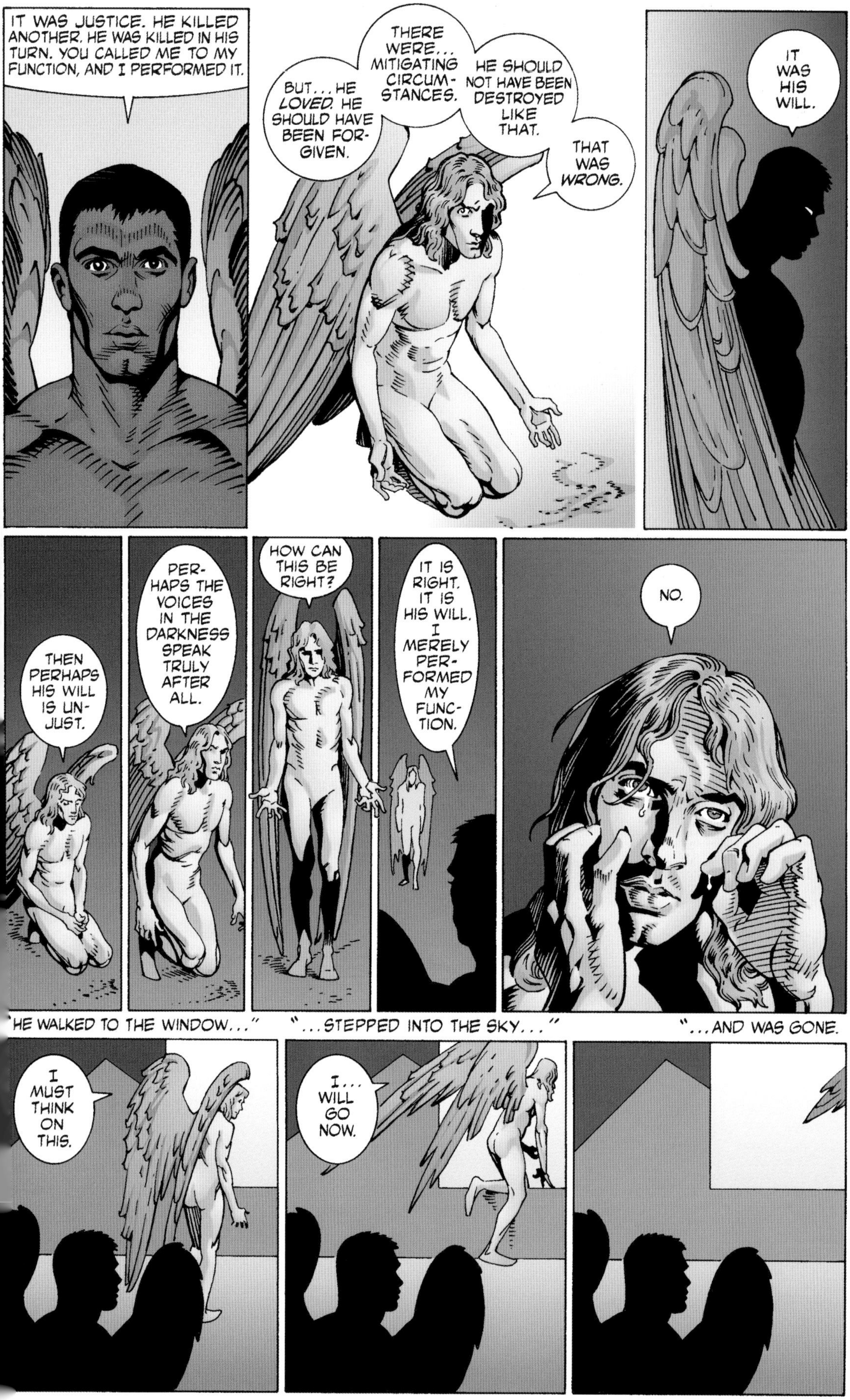
IT WAS JUSTICE. HE KILLED ANOTHER. HE WAS KILLED IN HIS TURN. YOU CALLED ME TO MY FUNCTION, AND I PERFORMED IT.
BUT... HE LOVED. HE SHOULD HAVE BEEN FORGIVEN.
THERE WERE... MITIGATING CIRCUMSTANCES.
HE SHOULD NOT HAVE BEEN DESTROYED LIKE THAT.
THAT WAS WRONG.
IT WAS HIS WILL.
THEN PERHAPS HIS WILL IS UNJUST.
PERHAPS THE VOICES IN THE DARKNESS SPEAK TRULY AFTER ALL.
HOW CAN THIS BE RIGHT?
IT IS RIGHT. IT IS HIS WILL. I MERELY PERFORMED MY FUNCTION.
NO.
"HE WALKED TO THE WINDOW..."
I MUST THINK ON THIS.
"...STEPPED INTO THE SKY..."
I... WILL GO NOW.
"...AND WAS GONE.

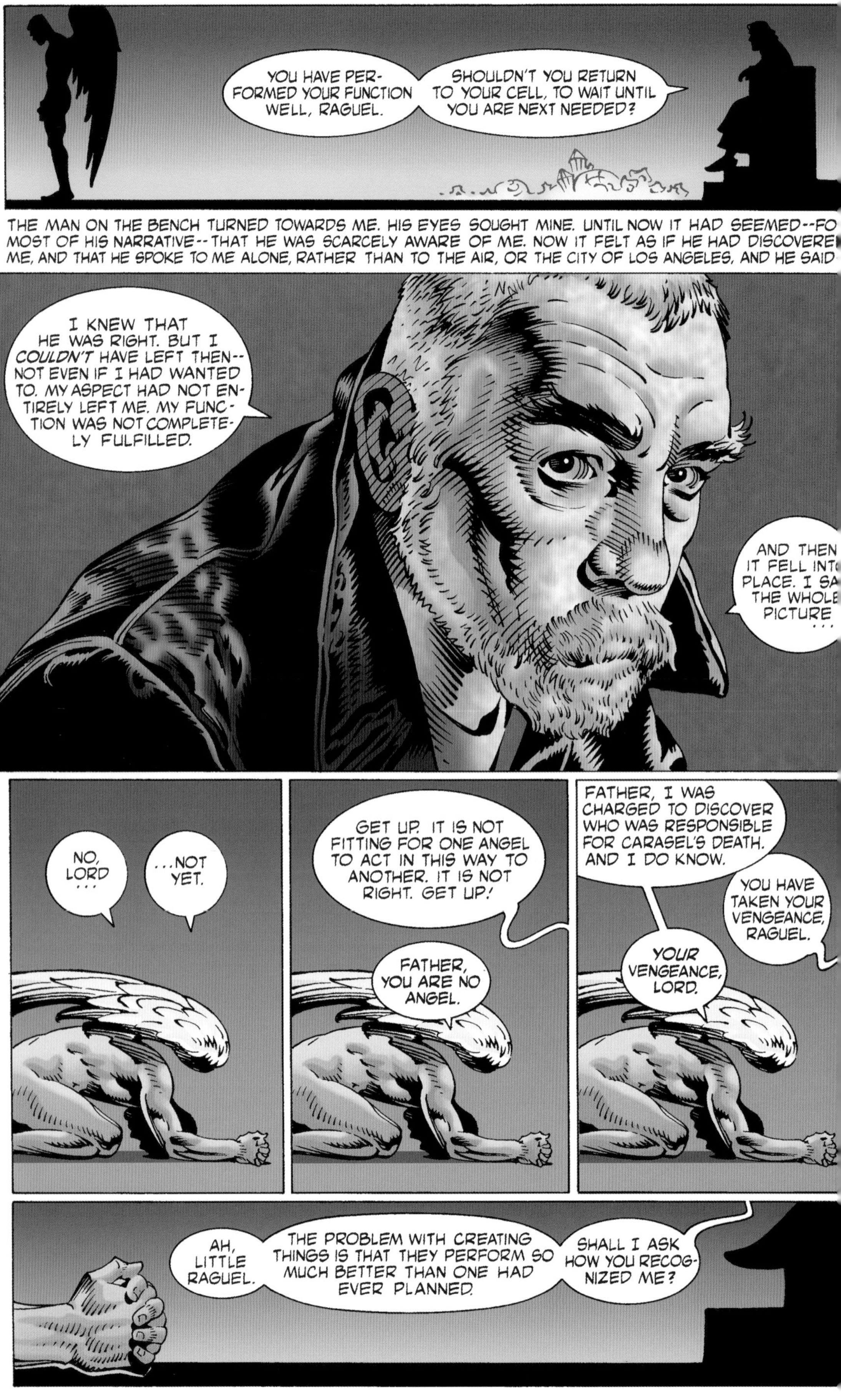

YOU HAVE PERFORMED YOUR FUNCTION WELL, RAGUEL.
SHOULDN'T YOU RETURN TO YOUR CELL, TO WAIT UNTIL YOU ARE NEXT NEEDED?
THE MAN ON THE BENCH TURNED TOWARDS ME. HIS EYES SOUGHT MINE. UNTIL NOW IT HAD SEEMED--FO MOST OF HIS NARRATIVE--THAT HE WAS SCARCELY AWARE OF ME. NOW IT FELT AS IF HE HAD DISCOVERE ME, AND THAT HE SPOKE TO ME ALONE, RATHER THAN TO THE AIR, OR THE CITY OF LOS ANGELES, AND HE SAID
I KNEW THAT HE WAS RIGHT. BUT I *COULDN'T* HAVE LEFT THEN--NOT EVEN IF I HAD WANTED TO. MY ASPECT HAD NOT ENTIRELY LEFT ME. MY FUNCTION WAS NOT COMPLETELY FULFILLED.
AND THEN IT FELL INT PLACE. I SA THE WHOLE PICTURE . . .
NO, LORD . . .
. . .NOT YET.
GET UP. IT IS NOT FITTING FOR ONE ANGEL TO ACT IN THIS WAY TO ANOTHER. IT IS NOT RIGHT. GET UP!
FATHER, YOU ARE NO ANGEL.
FATHER, I WAS CHARGED TO DISCOVER WHO WAS RESPONSIBLE FOR CARASEL'S DEATH. AND I DO KNOW.
YOU HAVE TAKEN YOUR VENGEANCE, RAGUEL.
YOUR VENGEANCE, LORD.
AH, LITTLE RAGUEL.
THE PROBLEM WITH CREATING THINGS IS THAT THEY PERFORM SO MUCH BETTER THAN ONE HAD EVER PLANNED.
SHALL I ASK HOW YOU RECOGNIZED ME?